Praise for *Break Through to Ye:*

G000094794

David B. Savage's *Break Through to Yes* provi< collaboration!
> —**Marshall Goldsmith**, Thinkers 50 #1 Lea_____
> Top 5 Management Thinker 2015.

Written in a manner that illustrates collaboration in action, *Break Through to Yes* shares decades' worth of knowledge and a structure that outlines what true collaboration looks like.
> —**David L. Milia**, MBA, CET, Associate Director, Centre for Corporate Sustainability
> / Energy Initiatives, Haskayne School of Business, University of Calgary

What a concept; a masterful book on Collaborative Leadership that is truly collaborative! This book will have you take a whole new look at how you operate in business. A MUST read.
> —**Teresa de Grosbois**, #1 International Bestselling author of *Mass Influence*

From the book's opening metaphor to its final appendix, David Savage's *Break Through to Yes* is filled with valuable insights, quotes and suggestions on why and how to see collaboration as the best (perhaps only) path to a successful and sustainable yes. Supported and enriched by many examples from his own work and the experiences of others, each section offers hope and direction with respect to how we can choose a different path in the way we work, communicate, problem-solve and interact with just about anyone.
> —**David Gouthro**, Facilitator and Past President of
> the Canadian Association of Professional Speakers

Significant improvement in communication, teamwork, creative thinking and problem solving can be realized by applying the knowledge David Savage and the many collaborators who shared their wisdom with David possess and share in this remarkable book.
> —**Don Loney**, President, Loney Publishing Group Ltd.

What if all of the stakeholders in your project, with competing interests and goals, had your back? What if all stakeholders can achieve their goals while supporting the goals of the others? With great insight and wisdom, David Savage shows us that leaders who use collaboration as their goal achieve just that. Don't mistake this book for just another "how to" missive. *Break Though To Yes* is a unique and powerful business tool that changes the culture of how to get things done.
> —**Jeffrey M. Cohen**, Esq., Mediator and Facilitator, Board Member of the
> Collaborative Global Initiative, Co-Chair of the Association
> for Conflict Resolution Ethics Committee

Too often individuals choose sides on issues such as climate change, resource management and land use as though they are sporting events where teams form to create win-lose outcomes. To overcome win-lose situations, many leaders ask people to "compromise," which leaves everyone feeling as though they lost something. Collaboration allows people to work together to find creative solutions and common ground so all stakeholders feel like winners. *Break Through to Yes* provides the steps needed to go from "compromise" to "collaboration" and create a nurturing environment to make optimum decisions.

—**Doreen Liberto**, AICP, MDR

Break Through To Yes is useful and sensible and the case studies prove to be helpful—especially in understanding group dynamics. So much of this book rings true.

—**Michael D Hill**, MD MSc FRCPC, Professor, Dept. Clinical Neurosciences, Hotchkiss Brain Institute, Cumming School of Medicine, University of Calgary

Everyone plays a leadership role at some point in their lives whether it's with family at home, peers at school, or employees in the workplace. David Savage's *Break Through to Yes* is an essential tool in the toolbox to help leaders truly understand how to create a culture of effective collaboration and when it should be implemented.

—**Don Simmons**, President & CEO, Hemisphere Energy Corporation

In *Break Through to Yes* David Savage is able to find the perfect blend of deep practicality and luminous vision. This blend makes the collaborative skills and knowledge offered in this book essential for any organization or individual looking to thrive in the 21st century.

—**Duncan Autrey**, Facilitator and Conflict Transformation Consultant

Savage makes collaboration concrete and shares unique perspectives how **we** can lead.

—**Donna Hastings**, CEO, Heart & Stroke Foundation—Alberta, NWT & Nunavut, Chair, Editorial Board, International Trauma Life Support

David B. Savage's *Break Through to Yes* is more than a depiction on the importance of collaboration. None of us accomplishes anything great on an island of one. This book will guide you unapologetically toward execution of your vision with direction of other trailblazers and game changers.

—**Camille L Nash**, MBA, Senior Executive Producer, VoiceAmerica Talk Radio Network

In this highly readable yet personal book, David Savage challenges us to bring collaboration to our work, to our nations, to our lives. Drawing on global experts in collaboration as well as on his own extensive experience, *Break Through to Yes* offers practical application of collaborative techniques, from assessing a situation through design and evaluation of collaborative practices. This book has gems of wisdom for anyone facing tensions from diverse viewpoints and challenges of change!

—**Jeanne McPherson**, Ph.D. in Organizational Communication, emphasizing Collaborative Leadership; McPherson Workforce Development

Break Through to Yes demonstrates that collaboration is a fundamental under-pinning to success in life and business and provides a clear understanding of how to create that foundation.

—**Stephen Smith**, Senior Advisor, National/International Stakeholder and Government Relations, Alberta Energy Regulator.

The intricacies of working with a group of volunteers can be fraught with dangers. It doesn't matter what the group is or what their ultimate goal or task is, the use of collaboration techniques is critical for success. With the rich resources David Savage provides in the pages of his *Break Through to Yes*, I know any leader can gain valuable tips and tools to succeed. If you aspire to leadership, this book is a MUST for your everyday reading. If you are already in a leadership position, the stories in these pages will be both an affirmation and a guidebook.

—**Allan Davis**, Past District Governor (2008-2009), Rotary International, District 5080

Break Through to Yes is packed with applicable and actionable wisdom every manager and leader can use.

—**Susan MacKenty Brady**, Author, *The 30 Second Guide to Coaching Your Inner Critic*

Break Through to Yes by David B. Savage is a break through in how businesses can lead at the next level—growing skill and competency in collaboration! Learn how to maximize collaboration in your organization from other high performing leaders in David's new book.

—**Dee Ann Turner**, Chick-fil-A, Inc.

Break Through to Yes is an important book for our times. Dave Savage's powerful tools will offer all readers renewed relationships and peaceful solutions to perplexing conflicts. I strongly recommend reading this book and applying Savage's advice for collaborative alternatives and "yes" agreements.

—**Dr. Joan Goldsmith**, co-author of *Resolving Conflicts at Work,*
Ten Strategies for Everyone on the Job, 3rd Edition

If we are to evolve and survive as a species, we need to learn how to collaborate and resolve conflicts with each other, both personally and globally. Doing so will require us to build skills in conflict resolution, strengthen our capacity for empathy and compassion, and recognize that, in the end, there *is* no "them" and "us," there is just *us*. Dave Savage has written a powerful and insightful book that offers useful techniques in collaboration and helps us see what we can do to make the world a better place. Read it, practice it, integrate it into who you are and what you do, and you will begin to bring that world into existence, from the inside out and the outside in.

—**Kenneth Cloke**, author of *The Dance of Opposites* and *Conflict Revolution*

Break Through to Yes

Break Through to Yes
Unlocking the Possible within a Culture of Collaboration

David B. Savage

elevate

For permission requests, please contact Elevate Publishing at
info@elevatepub.com

Editorial Work: AnnaMarie McHargue
Cover Design: Arthur Cherry
Interior Design: Kiran Spees

This book may be purchased in bulk for educational, business, organizational or
promotional use. To do so, contact Elevate Publishing at info@elevatepub.com

ISBN: 978-1-943425-15-0

All photographs and graphics copyright © David B. Savage

I dedicate this book and my work:
To our grandmothers and grandfathers.
To our granddaughters and grandsons.
To all who believe leading for "we" is greater than leading for "me."

And

To you, the reader, who is part of this paradigm shift from top
down to collaborative leadership,
To the 100 plus people around the world that have provided me
with their wisdom for this book,
To the 45 guests from around the world from my Internet radio
show and 15 podcasts,
To my family and especially my grandchildren and
To our shared future.
You teach me and, with collaboration, we create our great future by
working together better.

Contents

Prologue
Together a Forest

We stand together in this natural space. We are up to 150 years old. But we are young. We have tiny wild flowers and moss at our feet. We have a wetland as our close neighbor. We have deer, elk, bear, moose, cougar, ants, worms, gray jays, osprey, bald eagles, loons, bats, painted turtles, squirrels, caterpillars and lichen. We are alive. We are healthy. We are green. The air is fresh. We are Tamarack, Ponderosa Pine, Fir and Birch. With our neighbors, we are an ecosystem. We are together a forest.

Far down below our crowns, we notice a man with a chain saw. He brings pain, anguish, death…some of our family fall, are cut up and hauled away in trucks.

As rough roads are cleared more trucks come with earthmovers, more men and more chain saws. Our rich, green, mossy forest bed is scraped away by noisy, smelly machines. Rock and crushed gravel begin burying our nutrient-rich soils. An ugly, rectangular, grey tin mobile home is trucked in and set down where members of our family once stood so proud, so green and so in community. That large grey tin box is set so the humans can sit inside to view our wetlands. Our roots and ecosystem are destroyed to make room for the humans, their house and road. The wetlands now, too, are being poisoned by the pollutants seeping from this devastated site.

Powerful 80-mile-per-hour winds blow tonight from the south. Together a forest stands to protect our ecosystem. We know this and usually withstand the wind with ease. Yet, we have lost some of our strength. There are missing trees in our forest. The loss of those that have been cut down have lessened our ability to withstand the strong wind. We bend. When we bend in the wind, we bend too far into those blank spaces. Our trunks are cracking. A few of us crack open and splinter. A number of us fall. This is a night of fear like none of us have ever seen before. We tighten in our fear. We grieve for those in our family members that have cracked, broken and fallen. So much damage suffered by us and by those that caused this.

In the morning, humans burst forth in anguish and anger. . . and more chain saws and more earth moving. What was once our forest is now reduced to fewer than half the trees and ecosystem of a few short months ago. Can't these humans see what they are causing? Why do they not look up to us? Instead they look only at the damage to what they see as their own property.

Powerful fall winds blow yet again in the valley below the majestic peaks of the Rocky Mountains. In mere weeks we are no longer together as a forest. We Tamarack, Ponderosa, Fir and Birch are now stressed, separated and at risk. More of us fall tonight. For many, our community of 150 years is now reduced from prosperity to a horrifying survival mode.

The trucks return and get stuck in the gravel and mud that, a short time ago, was lush undergrowth. And, now, more trucks dumping gravel across the barren acreage that was once our forest. The wetland is in pain. The new high fence around the perimeter of this lot now interferes with the deer, bear, cougar and other wildlife that used to live and pass through this land.

The humans purchased this land for the beauty and natural environment here. Through their self-centered focus, ignorance and disrespect, we are no longer holding together as a forest. We trees did not fight back. What could we do when our root systems and entire ecosystem we helped support were so tragically and selfishly damaged. Many trees simply fell. We are now a gravel pit, with a trailer, trucks, fence and a very few Tamarack, Ponderosa Pine, Fir and Birch We hope that over the next 150 years, we will recover this ecosystem, but few of us believe it. This ecosystem is our collaboration. In the wind we hear more chain saws repeating their devastating mistake down the road. We wish these humans could bring us into their consciousness. We wish the wildlife had a presence here as well. Where are the humans that could have informed these men? Where is the collective wisdom? Why must we be isolated and then damaged. We dream of change.

This is a true story. This tragedy took place near my family cabin in the Rocky Mountains of British Columbia, Canada. Trees collaborate in nature, but have no knowledge of collaboration in the face of human destruction.

Humans collaborate and can learn together to change what seems to be tragic, inevitable consequences.

My wife, Lise, has been a professional forester and Supervisor for Compliance and Enforcement for the British Columbia Ministry of Forests, Lands and Natural Resource Operations. One of her many responsibilities has been to hold companies and individuals accountable when they damage the environment out of either ignorance or intent. Several years ago, she had charged a logging company with illegal tree harvesting beyond the boundaries of their permit area. The company management fought back. Her response included, "I am charging you for the value of a number of trees that have been destroyed. We assess the value of the timber in these matters. But what is the value of a tree in a forest? That is far greater than looking at a tree as a lone entity. Shall we go there?" The company paid the fine and started to look at ecosystems in a more holistic way. They started to realize the gains they may create by practicing a much more sustainable and collaborative culture in their organization.

Like trees, we are a forest together. In this forest, this earth sustains and challenges us. The actions, judgments and projects of others affect people and forests around the globe. How we collaborate determines the quality of our lives and the quality of our lives determines the ecosystem of human relationship on this small blue planet. By learning better collaboration skills and practices, we may become a more sustainable species. My intention is for the reader to become far better at communicating, engaging, creating, developing trust and holding accountability with others in their organization, community and family—and within themselves.

Too often, teamwork and direction consists more of manipulation and one-dimensional directives than collaboration and leadership. Our forests turn to barren land after the winds blow us down one by one. We must come together and learn how to lead from a collective perspective. One that honors the quality of life for ourselves, our families, our organizations and our global relationships. Together, we must learn to dream of a healthy economy, environment and community.

The family that was responsible for cutting down the trees near our cabin simply wanted to build their own beautiful home. But they gave little thought to the community they were destroying and how that would come back on them. Conversely, poorly or inconsistently executed collaborations can also damage the community/organization. Each act, each project, each team and each organization must plan, execute and celebrate how they work together as a continuum. We are all in this together. We are a forest.

Introduction

We benefit from the perspective and expertise of others.
Jason Donev, Professor, University of Calgary, Alberta.

Today, our world, our nations, our communities, our organizations and our families are faced with complex challenges that present massive potential risks. Yet we are at a time in human history where we are more educated, better connected, and have at our disposal far superior resources than ever before.

Unfortunately, though, our future is being damaged by conflict, misunderstanding and misalignment of organizations and their leadership. We are plagued with lost productivity, wasted time and wasted physical resources resulting from limiting perspectives, distraction and hard-line positions.

I have had titles including Director, President, and Chief Operating Officer as a businessman since 1975. Over the years, I have seen repeated failures, sometimes with costs in the billions, effect organizations and their capital projects and operations. When a company starts making mistakes, tries to force its agenda on others or is in conflict with its stakeholders, people revolt. Projects get delayed in regulatory and community review for extended lengths of time and employees simply don't give their best because they do not trust the systems they work in and have no say in the processes or programs in which they are involved. The costs to organizations can be both internal and external disengagement, rejection by regulatory bodies and governments, impacted communities, damage to the environment, and more. Add to that a wide range of human costs including everything from depression, conflict, suicide, marital breakdown and career paralysis to the loss of the intelligence and vision of the brightest people in your business because they mentally check out when they come to work.

Look at lost productivity from lack of meaningful connectivity at work. Look at lost opportunities to grow and prosper. Look at the busyness that you as a leader suffer that distracts you from doing great work.

Leaders and organizations can avoid all of this energy sapping negativity to gain a key strategic advantage when they work together to build a culture of collaboration.

Even the hardest work (engineering bridges, practicing law, designing buildings, raising money and other professional activities) can be executed much more efficiently and cleanly once a leader builds a culture of collaboration. A culture based on leadership, negotiation, and conflict management capabilities works together to produce meaningful solutions within organizations.

Remember Monty Python's John Cleese and his great training video— *Meeting, Bloody Meetings*? Imagine, if you will, another video: *Collaboration, Bloody Collaboration*. Too often, a boss has a narrow and predetermined task he wants others to buy into. The boss, at times, is afraid of making decisions alone, so he calls a meeting. "We must collaborate to succeed..." he begins, oblivious to the yawns, sideways glances and grimaces.

Our systems and organizational cultures are not functioning properly. Our regulatory and legal system, too often fails both the proponent and the opponent. Why do we continue to waste time, resources and people on so many poorly managed projects? *Break Through to Yes* promises to deliver a method to make collaboration work for you and your company. With this book, you are guided to create the conditions that promote innovation and break through within and across your business and network. Seize this opportunity to join a movement of progressive, principled and successful leaders who are daily creating the conditions to promote innovation and breakthrough within their businesses and networks.

When I started to research this book and link ideas, my intent was to help leaders realize the innovation and power of collaboration. Now, I invite the reader to realize that collaboration is far more than just an event or series of events; collaboration is a culture. In fact, collaboration has become its own field of study, practice and evolution. We see leadership, negotiation, dispute resolution, team building, stakeholder engagement, sustainability and other topics as fields. Let us together explore the field of collaboration. And let's develop it not only as one of several tools the reader brings to their work, but rather develop this discipline of collaboration as our way of leading.

Now is our time to lead more powerfully, consciously and collaboratively in ways that will make our world a better place today and in the future. The very best company leaders will start making this essential shift now.

In the past, we said, "The sky is the limit." With collaboration producing multinational space exploration probes, we may say, "The universe is the limit." Ron Fraser, the Director of Learning Services, Alberta Bible College, Calgary, has this to say about collaboration:

> First we live in confusing times, made more confusing by the tendency of more powerful people to speak for supposedly less powerful ones. At every level of our human interaction, whether business, medicine, law, education, etc., why not discover the actual interests that people have? Why not discover clarity by inviting real people with real interests to use their own voice? Collaboration levels the playing field by reducing the confusion created by power. Second, collaboration is a behavior, even a liturgy, that holds profound promise in shaping the deepest desires of human flourishing, the desire to love and be loved ... Collaborative habits can set the table for some of these primordial longings that make us truly human. The third reason is the hope that collaboration holds for learning. If finding and using one's own voice has anything at all to do with personal transformation (learning), then collaboration holds essential keys. The practice of putting into words, articulating what we mean, reshapes our horizons. When we speak, and hear others, our worlds move! The fourth reason, and perhaps the most important one, is that collaboration can become not just a practice but a way of being and becoming.

Leadership can connect the people within your organization, as well as across the world, in ways that have not been possible until now. Leadership is also about connecting with self. Are your actions and communications in alignment with your values? What values does a collaborative leader hold? Are you in coherence between your head and your heart? Do you lead from your heart and your whole intelligence? Do you see your purpose as getting the right things done that serve the whole?

As a conscious leader, what is your answer to:

A) Who am I?

B) Who are we?

Take some time to think about this. Your answers, as they are expressed in the moment, and as they evolve over time, inform your vision, purpose, community, actions and relationships. These questions were front of mind as a collaborative effort took shape among one hundred peers from around the world, who contributed their wisdom to *Break Through to Yes: Unlocking the Possible within a Culture of Collaboration*. Together we will take our awareness, curiosity and decisions to a much more profound and successful level.

> Remind yourself that if you think you already understand how someone feels or what they are trying to say, it is a delusion. Remember a time when you were sure you were right and then discovered one little fact that changed everything. There is always more to learn.
>
> *Difficult Conversations: How to Discuss What Matters Most by Douglas Stone, Bruce Patton, Sheila Heen (Douglas Stone, 2010)*

I have written this book:

1. To evolve the discipline of working together

2. As an invitation to understand and implement essential collaboration

3. With a focus on the role and responsibilities of current and future leaders in organizations

4. To provide leaders and managers with insights on when and how to collaborate

5. With a series of short chapters that can be easily read by busy people on

   a. What is not working in our relationships, and why

   b. How to know (assessments and tips provided)

   c. Stories that offer a vision of collaboration

   d. The 10 Essential Steps to Collaboration

5. To offer wisdom from a global perspective by sharing the advice of collaborators.

After you read this book, I hope that together you and "we" will grow our insights and expertise by creating a movement and sharing our ideas and stories with others online and in person. See the appendix for further information about this and other highlights of the book.

"Things will get a lot worse before they get better" is a too-often-heard phrase in business, not for profits and government. I have written this book as an antidote.

PART ONE

Why I Believe in the Urgency of Collaboration

Collaboration is an opportunity to amplify the power
of the relationship—with self, with others, and the world.
*Kerry Woodcock, leading change and collaborative
innovation specialist, Calgary, Alberta.*

" We face a host of systemic challenges beyond the reach of existing institutions and their hierarchical authority structures. Problems like climate change, ecosystem destruction, water shortages, youth unemployment, and embedded poverty and inequity require unprecedented collaboration among different organizations, sectors, and even countries. Sensing this need, countless collaborative initiatives have arisen in the past decade—locally, regionally, and even globally. Yet more often than not they have floundered—in part because they failed to foster collective leadership within and across the collaborating organizations."[1]

At every level, organizational leaders are looking for innovative solutions to optimize skills, perspectives, teams and ways of working together. They are unsuccessfully attempting to utilize the traditional divided structures they have relied on to date to address the ever increasingly challenging and complex environment they operate in. From individual families through to the American government and military, collaboration is seen as a solution. I see a collaborative culture as one that includes innovation, diversity, inclusivity, and analysis, all of which produce a successful outcome.

Collaboration has its place. Sometimes it is not the right tool for a given situation. How can we know when collaboration in its appropriate form is the right solution for the situation and when it is not? As a leader, you need a variety of tools to apply in different situations and with different people. As a collaborative leader, you will build the full and aligned tools and strengths within your organization.

"The first thing that's misleading is that there is a single thing that is known as collaboration. We can certainly think of it as singular but we can also think of it as having a kind of infinite number of manifestations. There are small-scale collaborations, which we engage in every time we have a conversation. There are larger collaborations that we engage in in communities and families.

"What we have a hard time I think imagining is how far exactly this can go. What is the deepest level of our collaboration? What's the highest achievement that we can make in this field? I think when we begin to think in those terms, we begin to see all of life completely differently," Ken Cloke, founder of Mediators Beyond Borders, on David B. Savage's Break Through to Yes with Collaboration Internet radio show and podcast.

I believe that for emergency response teams and the military, command-and-control leadership is necessary. My brother, Bob Savage, was deputy fire chief in the city of Kelowna for a good part of his career. Bob has a strong "take charge" personality (he originally got this from our father, which he honed during his career). I believed that a fire chief/site commander must be very much a top-down leader. When I put my belief to both Bob and, years later, to Bernie Fitterer, a former fire chief in Regina, Saskatchewan, they both gave me basically the same answer. When you are on a fire, you must be clear, concise, practiced and in charge. And the way you get your men and women to follow your orders is to build them as a team months and years in advance. In essence, you earn the right to command by being a collaborative leader.

So, let's look at the American government and military. If there was ever an image of a "get in line soldier and do exactly as I command," one would think this must be it.

In February 2014 the United States Government Accountability Office published a *Report to Congressional Addressees (GAO-14-220) Managing for Results; Implementation Approaches Used to Enhance Collaboration in Interagency Groups.* The Report found that "[m]any of the meaningful results that the federal government seeks to achieve require the coordinated efforts of more than one federal agency, level of government, or sector. The GPRA Modernization Act of 2010 (GPRAMA) takes a more crosscutting and integrated approach to improving government performance. GPRAMA requires that GAO periodically review implementation of the law. As a part of a series of reports responding to this requirement, GAO assessed how interagency groups addressed the central collaboration challenges identified in its prior work of 1) defining outcomes; 2) measuring performance and ensuring accountability; 3) establishing leadership approaches; and 4) using resources, such as funding, staff, and technology."[2]

If you, the fire department and the American government, seek to reach objectives through collaboration, then let's understand that collaboration, similar to leadership, negotiation, conflict management and strategic planning, is a field that requires serious study and understanding.

The Future Depends on Collaboration

Getting the people of the world to live in harmony will never
happen until we learn to get along and understand that everyone
has a different goal, but we are all one people together for life.

Colin Campbell, President, Guidance Planning Strategies Ltd.,
Cranbrook, British Columbia.

I have a wife, children, grandchildren, friends, peers, colleagues, a number of
organizations and an earth that I care about. And I care about the future.
I am a lifelong student of how to get the right people in the right place with
the right information in the right mindset to figure out how to conquer challenges and solve conflicts together. After thirty years as a negotiator, conflict
manager, leader, liaison and business developer in the Canadian petroleum
industry, I can say that I have invested thousands of hours (volunteer, association and corporate) to building awareness, capacity, round tables, organizations and success through working together.

I am also a serial entrepreneur, connector and coach. I made the decision to
leave my very select and trusted group of men and women that helped me create,
build and sell small oil and natural gas companies together. We committed the
next thirty years to helping leaders, organizations and youth to come together
in more agile and innovative ways. I removed my safety cable and jumped off
the ledge. Since 2005, I have worked with leaders, teams and organizations to
build their skills, businesses and deal effectively with this increasingly challenging and complex business environment. I, also, do the same on a number of key
volunteer boards and causes. My interests are wide and diverse:

- Here is a week (this week is from April 2015) that is typical for me:

- Negotiate on behalf of Hemisphere Energy with a multinational oil company to acquire an underdeveloped oil play near Jenner, Alberta

- Speak on Collaborative Leadership in Fernie, B.C.

- Coach a next-generation business leader on being clear on his values

- Participate in a Heart and Stroke Foundation Alberta Research evening event

- Work with ʔaq'am Community Enterprises to break down the economic development barriers between Indian Bands and First Nations

- Represent eight landowners with wilderness land and cabins north of Blairmore, Alberta to push back against an Australian coal strip mining company and to consider a renewable energy initiative

- Co-host a Canadian Association of Professional Speakers Fast Track group on business development and marketing, and

- Of course, write this book.

I believe in oneness. I believe in balance. I believe in diversity. I believe in conscious capitalism. I believe in accountability. I believe in working together. The working title of this book was One Yes. "In Chinese philosophy, yin and yang describes how apparently opposite or contrary forces are actually complementary, interconnected, and interdependent in the natural world, and how they give rise to each other as they interrelate to one another. Many tangible dualities (such as light and dark, fire and water, and male and female) are thought of as physical manifestations of the duality of yin and yang. This duality lies at the origins of many branches of classical Chinese science and philosophy, as well as being a primary guideline of traditional Chinese medicine. This duality is also a central principle of different forms of Chinese martial arts and exercise, such as baguazhang, taijiquan (t'ai chi), and qigong (Chi Kung), as well as in the pages of the I Ching written in 1,000 BC. Yin and Yang can be thought of as complementary (rather than opposing) forces that interact to form a dynamic system in which the whole is greater than the assembled parts. Everything has both yin and yang aspects (for instance shadow cannot exist without light). Either of the two major aspects may manifest more strongly in a particular object, depending on the criterion of the observation. The yin yang shows a balance between two opposites with a little bit in each."[3]

In fact, in 2008, I designed my corporate logo to include the yin and yang and "S" for Savage to represent holding of the whole.

Here is my challenge to you:

Reflect on the ways and behaviors in your leadership that you integrate the whole.

Reflect on the ways and behaviors of business leaders that do not integrate the whole.

Reflect on your beliefs on what the outcomes of both approaches most often create.

What are you mindful of based on these reflections?

How might you change the outcomes of your business decisions and initiatives by utilizing a more holistic approach to collaboration?

Collaboration and Sustainability

Collaboration is one of the most misused words today. It is thrown
out in conversations without regard to what it actually means.
Rod McKay, Chair, Heart and Stroke Foundation of Canada, Calgary, Alberta.

n 2012, when I started to research and write about collaboration, it was a
concept that sometimes popped up in conversation or in the media. But now,
only a few years later, as I present workshops on Collaborative Leadership, I
offer participants this challenge: If they can go twenty-four hours without
hearing the word "collaboration," I will refund their entire registration fee.
No takers so far. Listen to conversations, politicians, news broadcasts and
read social media and "collaboration" is used like some type of medical salve
for all our challenges. I suggest that few of those using the word know how to
collaborate well.

As leaders in organizations, there are two words that bring power to our
leadership. These two words—collaboration and sustainability—are misun-
derstood and misused. Rather than being embraced as a key to our success,
these two words repel many. With this book, however, I stand for the power
they bring. Next time someone you are in communication with uses the word
"collaboration," ask them what that they think the word means and in what
context they are using it. That is a real learning and creative conversation. As
you have these conversations, I invite you to contact me to share your wisdom.
I want to build a tool kit for best practices in collaboration and leadership.

Games

Ask yourself, does collaboration mean
that everyone must agree with everyone else?
David Milia, Associate Director, Centre for Corporate Sustainability/Energy
Initiatives, Haskayne School of Business, University of Calgary, Calgary, Alberta.

Finding Your Truth

Consider the social media and coffee room talk you've engaged in recently. Are these helpful collaborations or merely a rehashing of the "outrage of the week?" When I join in the judgment sessions on whatever is the outrage of the week, I miss the opportunity to connect, learn and be part of a solution. Consider what is possible. Consider what I call the "Collaboration Game" as a method of building your leadership and organization.

In 2015, a friend of mine in Boston shared on Facebook an environmental group's headline and photo warning the world "a tar sands pipeline spill by BP threatens 7 million people in Chicago. We must stop the tar sands and BP." Interesting. I Googled this and found nothing in the news. I posted a comment on my friend's Facebook share. "I have searched this on the Internet and have not found any such story. Where did you find this?" Her response: "I saw this post and feel I must be part of the solution and stop the tar sands and BP!" My reply: "I understand how you feel, but where are you getting your information?"

"From the Facebook post that X broadcast," she asserted. I responded, "I have friends that work for BP across North America and in the Canadian oil sands. I also have many friends who are deeply concerned about the environment, including water. Some are the same people. Would you be interested in forming a conversation with all of them to learn together about how we can best protect the earth's water supply?" Her Response: "That would be good. How can we do this?" My answer: We have all the technology, connection and wisdom we need. We can do this by forming both one-time and ongoing conversations, debates and collaborative strategies that examine great challenges and opportunities from a variety of perspectives.

Too often social media is anti-social media. Too often, what is true in a story is lost. The activist group that put the emotional trigger words "BP, tar sands, threaten millions…" together in one headline is very good. Marketing and influence-making in today's distracted and fast-moving world rely heavily on emotional engagement. Trouble is, throughout history the emotional triggers that are felt but not questioned, have got mankind into many deadly wars and disgusting prejudices.

Imagine a new game: a conversation that each of us practices every time we meet outrage or prejudice. You can play today when you encounter a person telling you something that is clearly tinged with "We must take action!" This may be anything where the communicator is certain the other side/opponent/ enemy is wrong. Examples are far ranging and you will find a great many. They may include public health care; oil fracking; professional sports; renewable energy; right vs. left; green vs. greed. The list is endless.

Instead of agreeing with one side or the other, allow yourself to engage in the simple game that can take five minutes or 50. The simple rules are that you act in truth, respect and curiosity. Here are 10 steps to playing the "learning together" game:

1.   Select a hot topic

2.   Seek agreement on how each of you will play this game

3.   Have at least three debaters each taking different positions

4.   Debate fairly and passionately

5.   Identify what is keeping you from agreement

6.   Identify what you need to know

7.   Identify how you will find that out

8.   Establish a plan to find out your truth

9.   Check back in once you complete the fact finding, and

10. Celebrate your collaboration and learning together.

Most often, do the Collaboration Game in a short period of time. For example, when pressed for time that you must complete the game in ten minutes, move beyond the debate within the first five minutes or else you will stay stuck in the debate without learning. In a 10-minute game, use your smart phone to call a friend, check the Internet or use whatever research sources you can to provide better information for the debate. Engage a third person because there is always at least a third perspective that is not considered.

Take a hot topic in the news and in conversations, host a virtual meeting with your network and play the game. I know that you will benefit from learning more and feel a higher degree of confidence to influence positive change. Today, you can be your own news organization. You can be the change you wish to see.

Hacky Sack Innovation

Want to engage and release people to be more playful and innovative? Pick a problem or an opportunity for your company or group, get everyone standing in a circle and give them the instruction, "From an outsider's view, what might you offer as the real reason we are struggling with this?" Have one participant throw one hacky sack (or bean bag or tennis ball) to another participant asking that question. With a smart phone record the responses as that hacky sack goes from one to another and each participant answers in a new way. Then add a request for participants to act out their answer in a characterization. Go from exploring reasons to interests to possibilities. Have fun. Laugh. Have a shared experience of exploring interests, issues and ideas. Innovate through acting and laughter.

The Essence of Collaboration

Collaboration, for me, is a lifestyle.
Rhonda Raven Neuhaus, Disability Activist and Life Coach,
Green Belt, Maryland.

I invited and received wisdom, advice and more from one hundred peers around the world on the topic of collaborative leadership. I asked each one to address three general issues: 1) The Number One. Reason to Collaborate; 2) The Number One Reason Collaboration Fails; and, 3) The Top Four Things That Effective Collaboration Requires. Eighty-eight contributors answered these questions. Another dozen provided their own advice in paragraph form. The research, compiled by Nova Scotian research assistant, Amanda Rogers, found the following:

Of the 88 questionnaire respondents, 55 were male and 33 were female. Sixty-two participants were from Canada, 14 from the U.S.A., one from Spain and one was from Australia. The participants hold a variety of positions among diverse professions, including titles such as (but not limited to): writer; manager; director; CEO; lawyer; practitioner; President; consultant; realtor; executive assistant; nutritionist; and professor.

The first global theme was the *#1 Reason to Collaborate.* The four organizing themes that helped to develop this global theme are working together toward a shared goal; personal and professional development; sustainability; and, other.

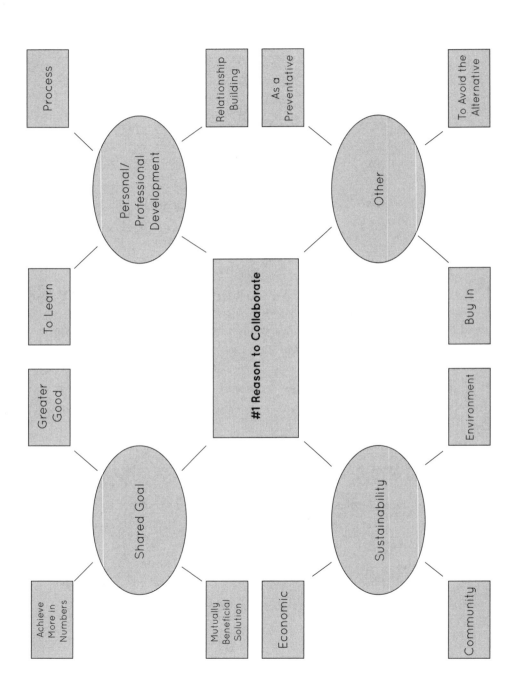

Working together toward a shared goal. This idea was the most frequent response to the question of what is the number one reason to collaborate. We found it 38 times. A significant number of respondents stated that we **will accomplish more working together than we will alone**; in fact, one collaborator stated that, "There is nothing more powerful than combining skills, experience, and creativity to create a synergistic approach." Garth Wiggill, the District Manager, Ministry of Forests, Lands and Natural Resource Operations, shares, "Focus on the people and the results will follow. Collaboration works on the premise that collectively we are a lot smarter than any single one of us." Collaboration invites us to transcend our own consciousness and be inspired into a new way of thinking and creating beyond what is possible alone.

Another common theme that respondents shared was the importance of working toward a **greater good**, to build a better community/sector/region together for the benefit of the whole. Tina Spiegel, the head of Spiegel & Associates of Sydney, Australia notes, "The collaboration relationship fosters a sense of belonging to something bigger than self and this is a human need that is sought in a world where disassociation is so easy to achieve."

Further, the collaborators spoke to the importance of a **mutually beneficial outcome**.

Nicola Carteret, journalist, author, Co-Founder and CEO of What's Life?, shares the story, "When collaboration shifts the power dynamics":

> I was once asked by a group of young entrepreneurs in the Middle East to facilitate a team in the design and implementation of the first-of-its-kind conference in the region to bring together young entrepreneurs from eight Arab nations.
>
> The reason for calling me in was to help negotiate and resolve some of the power dynamics between the Arab team and the European organization co-funding the event. The Europeans were insisting on designing a conference that would support their own vision and agenda in the region. The Arabs told me, "Although we appreciate the European support for this initiative, it's all about context. We are better positioned to understand the knowledge-transfer required for entrepreneurs in our region." But the Arab team had no cohesive vision and were feeling disempowered by negotiations with the Europeans. They couldn't afford to lose the funding, nor did they want to abandon the event. What to do?

When people within and across cultures don't share the same vision, purpose or goal, they are polarized by their differences. When people believe in a common vision, purpose, or goal, they are able to work together with love and no self-interest. A common vision ignites collaborative efforts.

So we set to work. First step was to consolidate the cohesiveness of the Arab organizing team, four men and two women. We agreed on a set of communication principles that would guide our discussions and work: listening to all ideas and acknowledging differences. I asked the team two questions: What's important to you in your life and work? What's motivating you to volunteer your time and efforts to create an outstanding event in the region?

Meisa, a recognized architect in the region said, "What matters to me is doing everything with love, with a big heart. If there's no love in the group, I can't be a part of it." Each one spoke in turn, articulating core values that would become the foundation for the cohesiveness of the group and ultimately for the event itself: love, kindness, simplicity, collaboration, beauty, integrity, creativity, and passion. Then I asked, "What kind of event do you want to create?" as I took them through a vision-walk exercise. As the team stepped into the future they visualized two hundred dynamic young entrepreneurs from Tunisia, Morocco, Algeria, Egypt, Lebanon, Palestine, Jordan, and Syria sharing creative ideas, collaborating, harmonizing, transferring knowledge and skills across three languages: Arabic, French, and English.

After clarifying the vision we then determined a simple and profound benchmark for each component of the event—from the knowledge sessions and welcome reception, to the food, gifts, and entertainment. The aim for each activity was to create a unique experience, "a WOW!" This vision was so clear, so compelling, so purpose-driven the team was mobilized into action, feeling it was easy to accomplish, "already done!"

The wonder for me, without over-romanticizing what took place, was witnessing the immense collaborative power that is released when heart energy is channelled towards the common good. Each person in the group was now 100 percent committed to turning their common vision into reality, all on voluntary time (outside their own busy businesses). I detected not a drop of self-interest, not one negative questioning of the actions or intentions of anyone else in the group, not a single negative word spoken about another team member. As Meisa had requested, there was only love in the group, a deep respect for each person's strengths and contribution.

Now here's the amazing part: as soon as the Arab group tapped into the power of "working with" as opposed to "working against," their collaborative energy shifted the overall power dynamics at the heart of their conflict with the European sponsors. And it took no time at all for transformation to happen. In a game-changing meeting, the Europeans detected the cohesiveness, solidarity, and collaborative energy of their Arab counterparts. Amazingly, without any need for negotiation (which I had thought was the next obvious step) the leader of the European team switched from being positional, and "stuck on his own agenda," to being open to hearing about what truly matters to Arab entrepreneurs in this specific cultural setting. The Arabs already knew the European interests and had found a way to include those interests in the event design. It was a win-win.

Then these six amazing men and women set about organizing sponsorship, speakers, hotels, transport, welcoming committees, hand-made gifts for the delegates, and a stunning cultural display (right out of their vision-walk)—an Arabian pathway through the conference venue where delegates could stop and hear rich poignant poetry dating back 800 years, a haunting flute and spine-tingling Oud (Arabic guitar). The event was hand and heart-crafted for the people by the people. It meant late nights, little sleep, and accommodating all the logistical obstacles that are inevitable in this part of the world. Yet I didn't hear a single complaint; each action was accomplished with a big smile.

It was one of the most beautiful acts of collaboration I have ever seen, a bit like poetry in action. A small group of dynamic people, aligned around a big hearted-vision, twelve hands lifting a mountain, becoming a magnificent force for mobilizing hundreds of others to contribute and participate. I kept hearing them say, "We are here to serve. We are here to create a WOW!"

And truly, once the conference began, that's exactly what happened.

Personal and professional development. Within this theme, it was frequently mentioned that **learning** was a top reason to collaborate: learning from others' gifts and skills, sharing and gathering perspective, and learning from the expertise of others will only benefit us and make us all more successful. Justin Brown, City of Calgary, Calgary, Alberta shared, "The reason I collaborate is to gather experience and wisdom. I will surround myself with people who have experience with certain situations. I do this especially when I am unfamiliar or uncertain with a situation or hurdle."

Additionally, several collaborators noted the importance of the collaboration **process**. Consider the thoughts of Dr. Nancy Love of the Pulse Institute in Edmonton:

> The collaborative processes seem cumbersome and time consuming especially when you are SURE you know what needs to happen. In my experience the process is most successful when the learning occurs within the group. Throughout the collaborative process they begin to understand the value of the dialog that brings people together and creates a TEAM before the project even begins. Relationships forged in collaborative processes are strong and respectful. You know where someone is coming from once you have been in a collaborative process with them. You know how to meet their needs and to express your own needs in a way that they can hear you.
>
> The outcome of a collaboration may be the same as it would have been if one person had made the decision. But the results are different.
>
> How a decision is made is often as important as what the decision is.

Finally, connected to the process is **team building and relationship building**; the cornerstone of collaboration. As Kerry Woodcock notes:

> It is in collaboration that I learn the most about myself, others, and the world. Collaboration is the ultimate coach, holding up a mirror to reveal the "me," "we," and "us" in all our kaleidoscopic beauty. Collaboration offers the creative and courageous space to weave the threads that connect, innovate, and lead change for a world of change.

Sustainability. Sustainability and financial restrictions were also noted as important reasons for collaboration. **Sustainability** is achieved by helping others along the way, learning how to grow and increasing your reach to continually improve. Spiegel shared her thoughts on sustainability:

> When the relationship is one of collaboration and not a power struggle or based on hierarchical power, it provides a workable framework with outputs that are sustainable. As it requires input from a variety of sources, more aspects of the task are brought to the light and considered from different perspectives. On a continuum the outcomes are more holistic and thus sustainable. The sustainability is reinforced by the process, and so the wheel of collaboration is fueled by the relationship of the humans to each other and to the issues they have confronted.

Financially, it is logical to collaborate when resources are scarce. O'Neil Outar, Senior Associate Dean and Director of Development at Harvard University, explains:

> There is a reality that external pressures drive collaboration. During times of duress, such as budget constraints, people and organizations are more open to collaborations because of their leveraging effect. In the philanthropic sector those pressures may include significant reductions in funding, the potential for new funding from a new source, or a disruptive technology, such as online education.

Other. Finally, there were a few other notable reasons cited for collaboration, including: a) to use collaboration as a **preventative measure** to minimize conflict and risk. b) to resolve issues before they reach the confrontational stage. c) because the alternative to collaboration is a process that is "hostile, combative, obsolete, counter-productive, and destructive." d) collaboration with the sole purpose of group buy-in.

The following diagram illustrates the frequency rate of responses, using a thematic approach, to the Number One Reason to Collaborate:

Frequency Rate of Responses:
Number One Reason to Collaborate

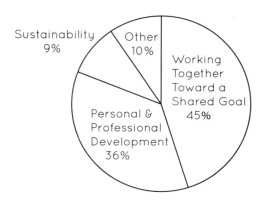

Sustainability
9%

Other
10%

Working
Together
Toward a
Shared Goal
45%

Personal &
Professional
Development
36%

The Number One Reason
Collaboration Fails

"Collaborations fail because the partners often have unrealistic expectations about how easy it will be. Working together is not the same as working independently. It is a marriage and the keys to success are the same as in the marriage partnership—finding someone who understands and can grow with you and persevere," O'Neil Outar notes.

The second global theme is the *Number One Reason Collaboration Fails.* The organizing themes that helped to develop this global theme are ego and personal agenda; disharmony during the process; suspicion and lack of trust; and lack of commitment and engagement.

Conversation in our culture is a competitive exercise in which the first person to draw a breath is considered to be the listener.

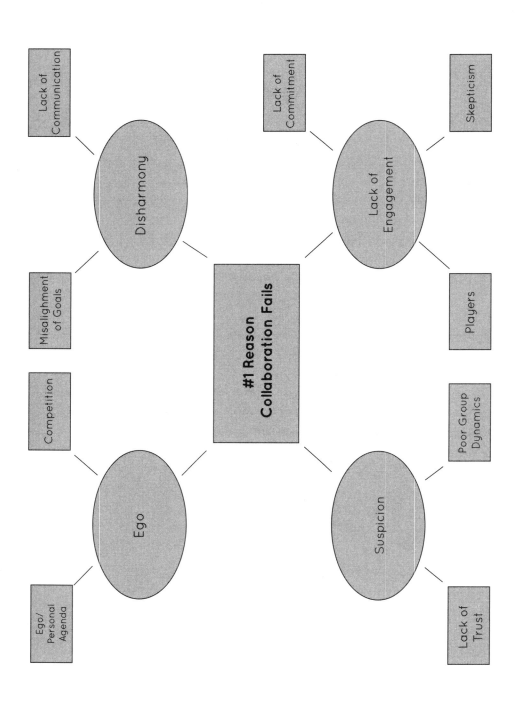

Ego. Ego, personal agenda and disharmony are three themes that had an equal frequency rate of 34. However, the word "ego" itself was the most frequently used term used in describing this global theme. When it comes to collaboration, Dave Struthers, chairman of the Cranbrook Chamber of Commerce, observes, "Individual egos and the 'what's in it for me' mentality need to be parked outside the door. The focus needs to be on the successful delivery of results across boundaries and between different organizations."

Nick Rubidge, President emeritus of the College of the Rockies, in Cranbrook, British Columbia, shares:

> True collaboration requires ongoing work and nurturing, building personal commitment between partners and between partnering institutions. Like a marriage, the partners to a collaboration must truly have the interests of their partner foremost in any discussion. Selfishness or self-interest, particularly when it comes to financial benefits, or even ignoring physic rewards, such as failure to recognize another's efforts will very quickly break trust and break up a collaboration even where financial benefits may still exist.

Disharmony. A **lack of communication** and **misalignment of goals** can quickly hinder collaborative processes. Communication is a multidimensional process. When even one aspect is missing a severe breakdown can occur. Examples of these aspects are listening, honesty, clarity, openness, sharing, confidence, safety and balance. Attorney Philip H. Schecter asserts, "Communication skills are very important. Listening and really hearing what others are saying and letting the others know there is comprehension of the communication is very important."

Spiegel describes what it means to listen:

> To listen is vital. In other words, we free our mind of previous ideas, beliefs and wow moments that say, "Yes, I have had the same experience and I know exactly how he feels." To listen means to take on afresh what a person is saying without the interference of judgment.
>
> To feel in your own body that you are being heard, the others have to listen. These two key elements, which are nourished by collaboration, are permanently linked.

Further, collaboration will surely fail if there is not a truly shared goal. Unrealistic expectations, undefined goal(s), unclear priorities, vague objectives and unrealistic timelines are all cited as reasons collaboration will fail.

Suspicion. A **lack of trust** and **poor group dynamics** were common occurrences within this theme. Secret agendas or withholding vital information to manipulate the process is not collaborative and will not succeed. Additionally, internal conflict and historical experiences create mistrust and obstacles to opening dialogue and effective communication. Henry Mead, Director Medical Therapeutic Area Leader Coagulation at CSL Behring, in Philadelphia, notes, "Sustainable collaboration is a process that functions like any relationship, the output is dictated by the integrity of the input. Above all else, trust and respect by all parties is critical for success." Coach Sherry Matheson echoes, "When a team has trust, respect and productive conflict, it creates safety so that members will speak up about their ideas or concerns and ask questions, take risks and learn from whatever failures or successes the team experiences."

Lack of engagement. **Lack of commitment, skepticism** and a lack of or **change in "players"** can all negatively impact collaboration. Shawne Duperon, CEO of Shawne TV, states, "The giving and receiving that takes place is not a tit for tat mentality. It's a deep yearning to truly be in relationship with someone you usually admire and want to support in THEIR dreams and mission." That is true commitment.

Mary Ellen and Lorraine Richmond, executive coaches, note:

> Collaboration is a risk. There is a risk that the partnership might be unbalanced in the time or resources that are contributed. There is a risk that the collaborative process or relationships will be used for selfish gain rather than for the greater good. There is a risk of unforeseen circumstances that might prevent the collaborative work from accomplishing its intended success.
>
> Yes, there is a risk. All of life is a risk. Yet, in my opinion, it is exceedingly rewarding to work hard together, through the processes of advancing something greater, to celebrating the desired outcome. After all, for every achievement great or small, the joy of the

celebration is that other people have participated in the journey and therefore, are able to share the celebration together. A party for one just isn't the same.

The following diagram illustrates the frequency rate of responses, using a thematic approach, to the Number One Reason Collaboration Fails:

Frequency Rate of Responses: Number One Reason Collaboration Fails

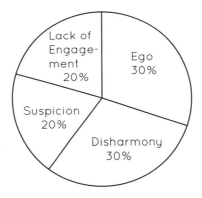

The Top Four Requirements of Collaboration

First time collaborators have not developed a trust in the process
to create the best decisions. We know the process allows the kind
of input and caution to create not only sustainable but regenerative
relationships and GOOD decisions but until someone has seen that
happen there is skepticism and concern. I have found two kinds of
concerns. There is the "BUT I'm the expert..." concern and there is
the "Why should I help them..." concern. Either will get in the way
of the deliberately gentle, honest, open and specific talk necessary to
ensure results and success from collaboration.

Dr. Nancy Love. Pulse Institute, Calgary, Alberta.

The third global theme is the *Top Four Requirements of Collaboration*. The organizing themes that helped to develop this global theme are: communication; commitment; shared purpose; and, diversity.

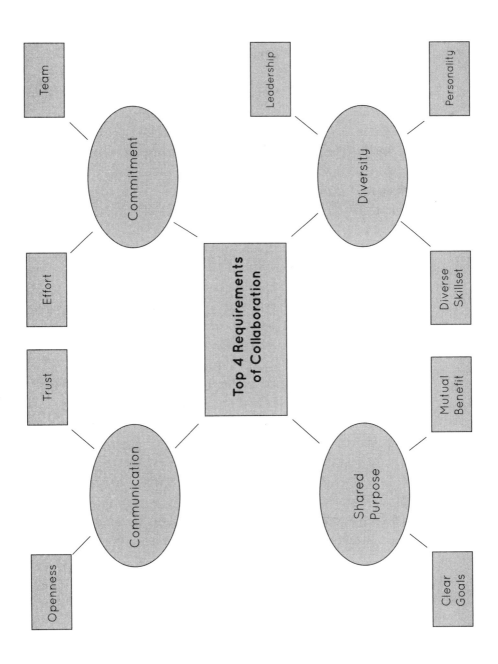

Communication. Open and effective communication had an overwhelming frequency rate of 56 as a top requirement for collaboration. Honesty was one word that was consistent throughout this area, as illustrated by Jackie Rafter, the President of Higher Landing Inc.:

> What many leaders fail to realize is that their thoughts and intentions are usually far more transparent than they realize—especially with social media and the office grapevine. It is for this reason that WHATEVER your leadership style is, being transparent, honest, up front and engaging the input of your team wins you far more brownie points and company loyalty than wearing your cards too close to your chest.

Effort and commitment. A common theme throughout was "willingness": willingness to partner and share resources; willingness to collaborate; willingness to be open to new ideas; willingness to give up being right; willingness to see things from the other person's point of view; and, willingness to set aside personal objectives. A genuine commitment and being open to new possibilities is critical for collaboration. Dr. Nancy Love describes it as:

> Readiness to collaborate—faith in the process if not also in the fellow participants

> Willingness to collaborate—everyone can see what might be in it for them.

> Able to collaborate—resourced for the time and energy at the beginning of a project and throughout to maintain the working relationship and create the best opportunities for everyone.

Shared purpose and clear goals. A recurring theme throughout this research is the importance of having a shared purpose and clear goals. A shared vision and unified view, mutually agreed upon goals, shared understanding of the desired outcome, deliberate intention and mutual benefit are all vital for successful collaboration. Denise Chartrand, President of Collaborative Engagements, says, "Collaboration is about people working together toward mutually acceptable outcomes. It requires consensus for sustainable results.

Consensus that all parties involved or impacted accept the solution as the best possible option within their current environment using the resources that are readily available."

Diverse personality and skillset. Diversity. Diversity of experience, expertise, personality traits/types, and knowledge are all cited as critical aspects of successful collaboration. David Milia explains:

> Can we collaborate when our selfish polarized views are in conflict with those we should be collaborating with? In business we have a name for a group of folks who all get along and have the same opinion on something, it's called GROUPTHINK and it is not good for business. I would put forward that true collaboration is a willingness to have a set of people with diverse competencies, world views, and experiences, with the added ingredient of wanting to pursue a clear and concise objective, come together in a safe space to talk about their position and how they hope to add value to reach that objective, even if it's not in alignment to others.

Aaron Parker, General Manager at Murrieta's Bar & Grill, shares a personal story that eloquently speaks to this theme:

> I was promoted to the General Manager position of a successful restaurant in Canmore, Alberta. I had spent a year and a half as the assistant manager observing the previous general manager operate his business. Shortly after I moved into my new position I began to meet with everyone on the team with a new mission. I asked them all, "What would you like to bring to this group?" Most, if not all, wanted the opportunity to do more than just be a server, hostess or cook. I found an individual with a passion for event coordination and gave her the opportunity to manage that aspect of the business. I found a gentlemen working toward qualifying for the RCMP (Royal Canadian Mounted Police) and with his strong ethics and values, promoted him to a closing manager with keys and safe codes, etc. I found a dishwasher with such a strong passion for the environment that he insisted he become our leader of recycling and thrives with the opportunity to "leave his stamp" on something successful. By

simply empowering these individuals within my group, we have collaborated into a fusion of power and as most would say, "many hands make light work." One person can't do it all, but together we can all get it done.

Leadership. Being the leader of a collaborative process is not an easy feat. This "champion" is expected to have the skill and ability to conduct a fair process. She or he is required to be flexible, committed and neutral. As Susan Brady, Executive Vice President of Linkage Inc., observes, "Collaborations need leaders. Or at least 'drivers'—someone who is more ambitious for the job at hand—or—is accountable for the end result."

The following diagram illustrates the frequency rate of responses, using a thematic approach, to the Top Four Requirements of Collaboration:

Frequency Rate of Responses: Top Four Requirements of Collaboration

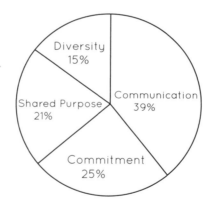

Gaps and Future Research

Collaboration is a dance of intimacy and thinking together and letting ideas emerge...The best collaborations are wider than the sum
of their parts and enable innovation and breakthroughs.
Amy Elizabeth Fox, CEO, Mobius Executive Leadership, Boston, Massachusetts.

Upon review of the responses to the Number One Reason to Collaborate,
only one collaborator stated "for buy-in" from others, even though
"buy-in" was stated as a necessary requirement of collaboration. This poses
the question of whether or not collaboration is initiated for genuine purposes,
or solely to get people on board with an idea. It would be important to learn
the following from the collaborators:

- Have you initiated/led a collaborative process?

- What was the purpose of the collaboration?

- Did you include participants who may not be initially on board?

- Did they get on board by the end of the collaborative process?

- What was the ultimate outcome of your collaboration?

- Was your initial purpose to collaborate altered through the process?

It is important to discover the *true* reasons behind collaboration. For
example, according to Ron Supancic, the founder of The Law Collaborative,
"We collaborate because the alternative is hostile, combative, obsolete, counter-productive, and destructive." However, there are many situations in which
we do not collaborate; in fact, we realistically do not have the funds, resources
or time to undergo a true collaboration for every decision that needs to be
made—this is why we elect leaders. So, do we create a hostile, obsolete and

destructive environment during those times in which we do not or cannot collaborate?

Further, a few times throughout the research, the subject of *how* we collaborate was noted as the most critical aspect of collaboration. For example, is the outcome of a week-long, in-person, facilitated collaboration as equally significant as a democratic email poll before a decision is made?

Although there was a pretty significant contribution from several colleagues, it would be beneficial to gain a larger sample, with a more balanced contribution from male and female participants in order to obtain a more global perspective on the topic of collaboration.

Charles O'Sullivan, Chairman, Hemisphere Energy Corporation in Vancouver, shares a personal story about collaboration:

> When I think about collaboration, I realize how it is so important both in business and in sport.
>
> During my teenaged years and then again at university, I was very much involved in competitive rowing. I rowed in both 4's and 8's, and always had very good rhythm and tempo, so I rowed as a Stroke, which is also called the Eighth. The Eighth sits in front of the Cox. Behind him are the 7, 6, 5, 4, who are heavier and the strongest in the boat. Toward the bow you have the 3, 2 and 1, who are progressively lighter, so the bow rides high in the water. The rowers have their backs to the finish line, cannot see it, and have to concentrate on what the Cox tells them. The Cox calls the stroke rate and the Stroke sets the rhythm and the tempo.
>
> When I equate rowing with business, I think of the Cox as the Board of Directors and the Stroke as the President. The remainder of the crew as the Management Team. All have to execute to the fullness of their ability, have to maintain balance and pay attention to what they are doing. Rowing races are very competitive and are usually won or lost by less than half a boat length. It takes total team effort to win, and if the Cox is not performing properly, nothing the crew can do can win the race. Though the crew vary in physical size and strength, each has to perform to 100 percent of their strength and ability.
>
> Of all the sports I have participated in, I think rowing depends on collaboration and teamwork more than any other. Nobody can hit a lucky home run in rowing.

PART TWO
The Discipline of Collaboration

Why Collaboration Is Misunderstood and Under-utilized in Business— and What To Do about It

[An important reason] to collaborate is to create from a group of individuals a "collective consciousness," whose pooled wisdom and creativity is synthesized into a shared goal.

Jeffrey M. Cohen, Mediator, Albany, New York.

Throughout the business world, on newscasts and in even in every day speech, the words "collaborate" and "collaboration" have become commonplace. The word is used to garnish the value of the speaker and/or their project. "We need to collaborate," and "Collaboration is good," they say. I would argue, however, that often collaboration is bad. Poor collaborations waste time and resources. Poor collaborations disengage people. Collaboration, too often, is used by weak leaders as an excuse for not leading. In fact, collaboration, too often, is used by commanders to sell what they have already decided.

My career is focused on building capacity in people to work together, decide for themselves and get things done well. I have sought out professional development as a mediator, facilitator and coach. These are powerful professions for our world and great skills for leaders. Like collaboration, too often, I hear leaders state; "I coached her" and "I mediated that conflict" and "we collaborated." These statements are disingenuous, ignorant and diminish professionals in those fields. Collaboration, to many, is getting together to work on something. This definition of collaboration is like defining architecture as "we draw stuff that gets built." Architecture is far more than drawing stuff. Would you lease office space on the 90th floor of an office tower designed by a person that draws stuff? Why would we skim the surface of working together when there is a growing tower of expertise and networks to guide you to create significant value, engage your people, realize new opportunities and create a strongly positive identity? Collaboration is a way of leading, an organizational culture and a power network.

When you Google "collaboration" you get at least 278,000,000 results. Seems there is a lot of interest in learning about collaboration. But what is collaboration represented as?

Merriam Webster defines collaborate as "to work with another person or group in order to achieve or do something." This could be the definition of a meeting or what a football team does. I prefer this definition:

"Collaboration is highly diversified teams working together inside and outside a company with the purpose to create value by improving innovation, customer relationships and efficiency while leveraging technology for effective interactions in the virtual and physical space." [4]

Let's make a joint proclamation that we value collaboration as a powerful way of leading. Collaboration isn't an act, it is the way we lead. To collaborate isn't simply to work together, it is an organizational culture.

Consider this Briefing Note I developed with Laura Hummelle, Ahead of the Curve Consulting, of Kimberley British Columbia, in 2015 to show several of the components leaders can use to develop themselves as collaborative leaders.

"In the past nine months, there has been an increasing awareness of the importance of collaborative leadership and change management in our region. Collaboration is often described by leaders as a key solution to the very real economic and community challenges we face. Yet, no current organization has taken the lead in supporting this change and form of leadership. Nor is there any organization that appears, on its own, to be agile, innovative and designed to work across the "silos" that currently exist.

Becky Pelkonen, an Economic Development Consultant, from British Columbia, Hummelle, and I are working to develop A Centre of Excellence in Collaborative Leadership and Change Management, which may serve as a non-partisan organization designed to:

- build the awareness and skills in collaborative leadership and change management,

- establish an ongoing series of training and coaching to provide leaders with support,

- realize the network of people and resources we currently have available to us, and

- move area priorities that have already been identified but are not yet being championed outside specific organizations and to create success through collaboration."

Do you choose to become a collaborative leader or call more meetings? How will you lead in the collaborative field of leadership?

The Value of Collaboration

In the general sense, there are always challenges. Every person,
every group, every community has a different set of agendas but
there's no greater feeling than when groups can come together and
collaborate on a particular project or program and
see that come to fruition.

Glenn Isaac, North Saskatchewan Riverkeeper, Edmonton, Alberta.

The Practice of Collaboration within an Organization

Don Simmons, President of Hemisphere Energy Corporation, Vancouver, British Columbia has put together an effective, talented and successful small relatively young team. With only eight employees and four part-time consultants, communication is strong and clear. Everyone has each other's back. When challenges and barriers arise, as they often do for small oil and gas exploration and development companies, the team gathers and together sets clear objectives, action plans and accountabilities. There is no divisiveness. A group of 12 people, with diverse expertise, solve problems together. Hemisphere is alert, agile and productive. Simmons, far more than most oil-company Presidents, understands the entire business and the importance of people and leads with integrity, inclusion and professionalism.

To be a good leader, then, we are required to hold our team, our company, our family and, especially, ourselves not only accountable for failures, but more importantly accountable to ensure that positive learning occurs and is shared. "Look at this. I screwed up. This is what I learned and here is how we can alter our course to achieve better results next time." This aspect of leadership provides a clear incentive and invitation to others. To fail to be accountable, to find out why we failed and to share this learning dooms others to fail similarly. To allow this is leadership negligence. Collaboration is learning together constantly.

My long-time business partner in four small oil and natural gas companies and one diamond mining venture is Bruce McIntyre. In 1996, Jeff McLean, a mutual friend and oil industry professional introduced us. After a long and in-depth meeting, Bruce and I agreed we must work together. Bruce asked, "Well, which one of us should be President?" I replied; "You have started the company already, have a great "Kennedy-esque" presence and have an incredible mind for detail. My strengths are negotiation, agreement building and stakeholder engagement. You be President and I will be Vice President, Joint Ventures and Land." When I later completed an interview with the company Chair, Wieland Wettstein, Wieland captured our collaboration completely. He said, "David, this will work very well. Bruce, will find us a lot of oil. You will capture the rights to it. And, our Chief Financial Officer, Michael Makinson, will never allow us to go broke."

We gathered several more talented oil industry peers and successfully built and sold the company for many times more than the investors put into it. Bruce, Wieland and I later created, built and sold Sommer Energy over a five-month period and again paid investors out multiples of their dollars invested. I trust Bruce, Wieland, Don and many others. When we collaborate, we work together very effectively. We used to joke that when we started to need procedure manuals, weekly meetings or our company name on any clothing, it was time to sell the company. While it is true that collaboration with trusted and respected peers is often far easier in small organizations than large, large organizations do have greater resources and depth of talent that make effective collaboration there potentially far more significant.

> There are circumstances where people don't want to throw the ball back. In those instances, you really have to deal with that. You call it a rogue in your midst. They can be destructive to the team. Those are the sorts of individuals that need to be weeded out and that's where collaboration doesn't work. I think that's a call that's often made by the person at the top. It's not something that you really can collaborate on.
>
> *Bruce McIntyre*

My Thoughts on Collaboration:

David L. Milia, Associate Director of the Centre for Corporate Sustainability, Haskayne School of Business, University of Calgary.

Personally, I find collaboration to be integral to how I define success. As someone who is driven to produce tangible results in every endeavor I take on, collaboration was something I needed to learn as the push for achievement can come at the expense of people. That is to say the "getting there" was originally more important to me than the "how we get there together" was. Over time, I have found that how a group of folks collaborates toward common objectives is more important, and tends to add more personal value, than the objective at all costs approach. This learning is founded on three major experiences I had over my career with collaboration. I call it "A Tale of Three Collaborations."

Tale 1: Collaboration in the Guise of Manipulation

The notion of collaboration is widely perceived and accepted to add value but seldom practiced properly. It is important to know when it is used as a means to manipulate rather than truly enable collaboration. I received this learning when I was a potential candidate for promotion at a major oil and gas company. I had pushed hard to manage certain risks the company faced based upon my direct area of accountability for the company. Through my efforts, I had instituted several controls that some leaders within the business units (BU) of our company perceived as too constrictive in allowing for their operations to meet the deadlines imposed upon them. My expectation at the time of hearing the first rumblings of misalignment was that we would meet to discuss what a win-win solution might be, given our differing accountabilities. What happened, instead, was a cloak-and-dagger invitation to a coffee by a senior leader who indicated to me that the company wanted to promote me, but I needed to show I could compromise and take a step back on my position to meet the needs of the BU leaders. This was followed by the idea that in doing so I showed I was a collaborative member of leadership. Now don't get me wrong, I was open to feedback to look for opportunities to meet both my accountabilities and remediate those of the BU leaders. But there was no communication or formal feedback, just a behind-the-scenes, semi-blackmail approach to have their accountability take precedent over mine without a conversation.

Takeaway: I learned that day what it feels like not only to have a lack of collaboration, but also have to deal with an ethical dilemma. Needless to say, this is not collaboration.

Tale 2: Competency-based Collaboration

As I became a leader who actually wanted to make an impact on the team I led, it became evident that I would need to learn from others. I began studying the Blanchard approach to situational leadership as one of my key areas of practice. This approach takes a lot of effort and requires the leader to conform to what his employees need to be effective, and more importantly, how to respect the area within which they are more competent than their leader. Which leads me to my second collaborative tale. Part of my job mandate dealt with managing multi-disciplines in the engineering ambit (mechanical, electrical, civil, and structural). In this example, I was accountable for a specification that dealt with ambits of electrical and mechanical engineering, but I did not have a proficiency within those disciplines that was as deep as the engineers who were on the team. At a meeting where a critical component of discussion was up for debate, the electrical and mechanical engineers of the team put forward arguments as to why their position outweighed those of their respective colleagues, and as a gap widened during the conversation the dialog descended into personal attacks on each other. As a situational leader I could tell this was not adding value to the task at hand and quickly adjourned the meeting to cool tensions down. I then had to weigh how to best deal with the issue given the criticality of the topic and resorted to situational leadership based on competency while remediating the feelings that had emerged. What did this look like? At the next meeting, I took my privileged position of accountability and expressed once again what the objective of the meeting was. I then pointed to the person on the team who had the most respected competency and breadth in the topic and indicated that if we got caught up in a personal tug of war, I would quickly adjourn and implement the recommendation of the respected competent colleague I had identified. This resulted in a calmer discussion.

Takeaway: I learned through this experience that collaboration is not easy and can quickly escalate into feelings of disrespect and attacks that don't help the team progress.

Tale 3: True Collaboration

Ask yourself, does collaboration mean that everyone must agree with everyone else? Can we collaborate when our selfish polarized views are in conflict with those we should be collaborating with? In business we have a name for a group of folks who all get along and have the same opinion on something; it's called "GROUPTHINK," and it is not good for business. I would put forward that true collaboration is a willingness to have a set of people with diverse competencies, world views, and experiences, with the added ingredient of wanting to pursue a clear and concise objective, come together in a safe space to talk about their position and how they hope to add value to reach that objective, even if not in alignment to others.

I wish I could say there are many examples of this, but I have only a few. One that is near and dear to me is with regards to enabling the future aboriginal youth of Canada. I come from oil & gas, have a business mindset and am not aboriginal. Moreover, I am not a subject matter expert in aboriginal relations, nor their history or traditional knowledge. All I bring is a heart to enable aboriginal youth in the areas where I have a competency, on their own terms, in order to meet their goals. In Canada, there is a high level of complexity around aboriginals and many polarized views. In looking at how I can add value in this sea of complexity, I have met several people who have a robust depth and breadth of competency and knowledge in this area, but are not necessarily aligned to business or my views/competencies. Does this mean we cannot collaborate? I have found that if a common area of passion/alignment/focus can be achieved, and we are willing to respect and recognize our counter-position as a valid position, progress can result.

In this example, looking to build the aboriginal youth of tomorrow is an area where many groups can align, with different competencies, experiences, and potential avenues. My humble part? To offer a clear picture of business, and of oil and gas, to any aboriginal youth who wished to go down that path. What can I achieve by collaborating and respecting my peers with other competencies and pathways? When I am exposed to an aboriginal youth who clearly misaligns to the areas where I can add value, I not only have a better understanding as to what could be another viable path for them, but also how to connect them to the person who can get them there. The ultimate result isn't always perfect, but does add value to the youth in question on their terms.

Takeaway: Listening to those we disagree with or who have knowledge in an area we do not can be hard and bite at our egos, but in the end if the objective is clear and both parties are passionate about taking positive steps towards that outcome, collaborating ultimately adds value to both of their endeavors."

The Practice of Collaboration
with Stakeholders

[Collaboration fails] when there is a lack of integration or contribu-
tion of all individuals in the community.
James Muraro, Geophysicist, Calgary, Alberta

All entities are "special interest groups." Companies, political parties, environmental organizations, news media, natives and communities all tend to narrow their perspective (i.e. biases) and energize their own prejudices to advance their personal interests. These interests may be capital projects ranging from thousands of dollars to billions of dollars. These interests may be to generate funds or votes. These interests may serve the organizations or collectives in many different ways. But each "special interest" tends to be communicated in black and white, good and bad, right versus wrong.

What methods might be more productive and meaningful than the dualistic argument? A good start would be to cultivate a personal awareness and take action in all our relationships, work and purchasing choices.

Throughout my career, I have sought to bring together diverse perspectives and expertise to identify and re-align people, processes, regulations and terms of engagement, so that the "good guys win" and the "bad guys" don't get rewarded for misbehaving. Far too often, our political, legal and regulatory processes favor those that seek power over justice and the public interest. Too often, the organizations with the power run over those that don't possess the same resources. Too often, special-interest groups run over the interests of the community. This is about what is right and how that is determined.

In 2000, while chairing the Calgary Chamber of Commerce Appropriate

Dispute Resolution Committee, I worked with a group of about 20 volunteers who sought positive, respectful and productive ways to manage growing conflicts between industry, communities, aboriginals and environmentalists. We modeled Essential Collaboration and each represented a part of every one of these supposedly separate groups. This group put together the Conflict Solutions 2000 Conference that brought together 125 people to learn and develop better ways of relating and working together. However, we received scant media coverage.

That weekend, the media, instead, focused on a man named Webo Ludwig. Ludwig presented himself as the little guy versus Big Oil. For some, Webo and his group were speaking their truth. For others, Webo and his followers were directly and indirectly linked to several bombings and the murder of a young woman. Webo was serving the Mediots no matter what "side" you took.

In 2009, I coined a new term: MEDIOTS. Mediots are those in social media, traditional media, politics, and the world who subscribe to narrow, exclusive, one-dimensional thinking, who cast fear, separation and misunderstanding in their pronouncements on current events and issues. Mediots are driven by and in turn drive our own reptilian brains into fast emotional judgements placing ignorance over intelligence.

Our conference Conflict Solutions 2000 was not news. We did not appeal to the mediots. Violence and hostility did. When we asked a Calgary based TV journalist, why the media ignored 125 people who were working together to solve these challenges and instead filled their content with conflict, we were reminded that "If it bleeds, it leads."

This conversation has been hijacked. There is a better path forward with a more complete perspective and new insights … Can you be a bridge to a better tomorrow? Can you lead without the bleeding? If a tree falls in the forest, does it make a sound? Today, if a person leads and there is no media or social media there, does it make a difference? If a tree falls in the forest and there is no one around, why bother? Because you matter, and together we are a forest.

Today every change, every incursion, every proposal, every leader is faced with passionate opposition. The Internet, education and democratization provide billions of people with information, a perspective, a judgment and a community.

Whether the project is wind turbines on a ridge or massive strip mining doesn't matter. People matter. People need to be heard. People need to listen.

Often today, we mistake passion for intelligence and commitment for ignorance. We act as if we live in a dualistic world of right and wrong, good guys and bad guys, heroes and villains and winners and losers. The biggest loser is what we didn't understand and what we failed to co-create.

We live in a world of one. When we act that way, powerful positive change occurs.

Within our World
(Sustainability and Social License)

Sustainability is reinforced by the process and so the wheel of collaboration is fueled by the relationship of humans to each other and to the issues they have confronted.

Tina Spiegel

Tough Mudder Leadership

We used to think we are separate, that it was every man for himself. We used to think our business was to cross the finish line first. We used to think we could know it all. Our challenges today seem much greater than yesterday. The challenges of tomorrow are expected to be greater yet. How will we meet these challenges?

I will tell you a story that links to my answer to our question on future challenges.

My son, Dan Savage, Lead Artist, at Infinity Ward, lives and works in Los Angeles. Last spring, Dan called me; "Dad, remember when I was five you started having me join you in 5k and 10k (3–6 mile) fun runs for charity? "Yes. Well, before you turn 60, I want you to join me in the first Tough Mudder in Canada. It will be at the mountain resort of Whistler, British Columbia and will cover 20 km. (12 miles) with 22 obstacles." As he had been in six Tough Mudders and qualifies in the top 5 percent in the world, I was both impressed and scared by his challenge. I replied, "Thank you for the opportunity. It will scare me into better fitness. Dan, you know I am a negotiator, so I must counter propose. I will participate in this extreme mountain challenge provided you will stick with me throughout the race and that you and I will hold hands as we cross the finish line together." "Agreed!" "Oh, and Dan, remember those 5 km (3 mile) runs when you were young?" "Yes." "You should also remember that I carried you most of the way!" "Ha!" I looked on line and read, "Tough Mudder events are hard-core 10-12 mile obstacle courses designed by British Special Forces to test your all-around strength, stamina, mental grit, and camaraderie." Obstacles are lovingly named Arctic Enema, Underwater Tunnels, Ball Shrinker, Firewalker, Trench Warfare and the Mud Mile. Better get to boot camp. This is a big challenge.

Late June, in the cold mountain air at dawn, we are in the bullpen at the starting gate for Tough Mudder. I am nervous. Holy s-it, the average person here is half my age, this course is up and down the mountain, through snow, ice, miles of heavy mushy mud, 3-meter (10 foot+) high, flat-faced walls to get over, ice cold water to swim through! The Navy Seal type starter is yelling and the metal music is pounding to get us ramped up for a grueling day. The starter yells through the bullhorn; "Look around you at the fifty people in this group. Your mission today is not to beat them. Your mission today is to make certain that everyone in this group completes the course." Hey, I am liking this more now.

And, sure enough, the challenges were very tough; the obstacles crazy, the mud oozed into my genetic structure and most everyone helped anyone else that needed help. With a very few exceptions and a few bypassed obstacles, we all completed the course. My son, the veteran of six, helped many others through this first event in Canada. Just before the finish line is Electroshock Therapy (where you run through up to 10,000 volts of electricity). As I steeled myself to get through, Dan grabbed my hand. After 20 km. (12 miles) and 22 obstacles, we ran through the bare electrical wires and crossed the finish line together.

That day with Dan is now added to our great life memories. This picture is also a reminder that I/we can overcome great challenges. How do we overcome great challenges? By collaboration. Remember, the elite special military forces (like Canada's JTF2 and the American Navy SEALs) put collaboration and looking out for one another far above the individual's pursuits. They do this to make certain their missions are successful and everyone comes back healthy. In the old days, we are led to believe, lone rangers and cowboys were the heroes. In the world of today and tomorrow, the cowboys will likely be killed.

Remember what the strong man at the starting gate in Whistler said; "Look around you at the fifty people in this group. You mission today is not to beat them. Your mission today is to make certain that everyone in this group completes the course." This course is live and our future.

The walls are getting higher for business. We will make our organizations a more positive influence on future generations. We will do this through awareness, collaboration, co-creation, leadership, accountability and our focus on all three pillars of sustainability (economic, environmental and social). We will profit from this shift. Our commitment is to educate, communicate and engage people at all levels of our organizations, industry and nation.

Will you participate in the extreme mountain challenge and opportunity? Or, will you be a bystander and nay-sayer? What are the consequences of both choices?

Think about your family, community and our planet 50 years from now. And now make decisions on your projects, investments, brand, relationships and impacts in service of today and 50 years from today. Together let's move from self-interest and "Green Washing" to Gifting to Our Future. How will you choose to have a more positive sustainable impact on your family, organization and community today and every day from now on?

Opening Ourselves, Our Organizations and Our Systems

Collaboration for me is a form of moving in life from Spirit,
verses ego and competition.
Rhonda Raven Neuhaus

In their book *Leading from the Emerging Future*, Otto Scharmer and Katrin Kaufer describe three "openings" needed to transform systems: opening the mind (to challenge our assumptions), opening the heart (to be vulnerable and to truly hear one another), and opening the will (to let go of pre-set goals and agendas and see what is really needed and possible). These three openings match the blind spots of most change efforts. These blind spots are often based on rigid assumptions and agendas and fail to see that transforming systems is ultimately about transforming relationships among the people who shape those systems. Many otherwise well-intentioned change efforts fail because their leaders are unable or unwilling to embrace this simple truth. [5]

Mindfulness is a holistic practice—mindfulness as to ourselves, our people, our systems and the communities in which we live and work. From each of these places, can I/we hear, let go of judgements and expectations and see possibilities greater than our own? According to *McKinsey & Company*:

> In the space of only a few years, companies in nearly every sector have conceded that innovation requires external collaborators. Flows of talent and knowledge increasingly transcend company and geographic boundaries. Successful innovators achieve significant

multiples for every dollar invested in innovation by accessing the skills and talents of others. In this way, they speed up innovation and uncover new ways to create value for their customers and ecosystem partners.

Smart collaboration with external partners, though, goes beyond merely outsourcing new ideas and insights; it can involve sharing costs and finding faster routes to market. Famously, the components of Apple's first iPod were developed almost entirely outside the company; by efficiently managing these external partnerships, Apple was able to move from initial concept to marketable product in only nine months. NASA's Ames Research Center teams up not just with international partners—launching joint satellites with nations as diverse as Lithuania, Saudi Arabia, and Sweden—but also with emerging companies, such as SpaceX.

High-performing innovators work hard to develop the ecosystems that help deliver these benefits. Indeed, they strive to become partners of choice, increasing the likelihood that the best ideas and people will come their way. That requires a systematic approach. First, these companies find out which partners they are already working with; surprisingly few companies know this. Then they decide which networks—say, four or five of them—they ideally need to support their innovation strategies. This step helps them to narrow and focus their collaboration efforts and to manage the flow of possibilities from outside the company. Strong innovators also regularly review their networks, extending and pruning them as appropriate and using sophisticated incentives and contractual structures to motivate high-performing business partners. Becoming a true partner of choice is, among other things, about clarifying what a partnership can offer the junior member: brand, reach, or access, perhaps. It is also about behavior. Partners of choice are fair and transparent in their dealings."[6]

Collaboration requires openness and hard work to transform systems. And in developing these systems, we develop trusted internal and external networks. Counter intuitively, ceding control over external networks and partnerships is a necessary component of effective innovation through collaboration.

In *Wikinomics: How Mass Collaboration Changes Everything*, Dan Tapscott and Anthony D. Williams explore what thinking differently, global thinking and co-innovation requires; being open (platforms, developers and thinking), peering (partnering), sharing (resources and ideas) and acting globally. "Engaging in collaborative communities means ceding some control, sharing responsibility, embracing transparency, managing conflict, and accepting that successful projects will take on a life of their own. This can be awkward for companies accustomed to command-and-control systems. It means learning new skills sets that emphasize building trust, honoring commitments, changing dramatically, and sharing decision making with peers."[7]

An Assessment for Your Organization

The two key aspects of collaboration are the ability to assert your opinion and the ability to cooperate with others.
Kathy Porter, Executive, Collaborative Global Initiative, Vancouver, British Columbia

How might you assess the state of your organization's collaborative ecosystem? Think of how beneficial an assessment would be that pertains specifically to your organization, the particular challenges and opportunities you face, your connection to your collaborative networks and where the strengths and weaknesses are what you will address. Consider this an evolutionary assessment that you check back to every three to six months. This will be an organizational success indicator. This will be a tool that your team, department, organization and network can assess from a "we" perspective.

I offer you an assessment. I invite you to customize it for your own organization, add/subtract aspects and continuously develop over time. The order of the aspects/questions/topics may be re-organized, prioritized or randomized.

In this assessment, I consider the elements of essential collaboration and the expertise of your network.

Rank your team, specific to one project initially, on a scale of 1 to 5 with 1 representing not effective and 5 representing very effective. I recommend you do this individually then combine the comments and average the totals. The order of the questions is meant to be random. A version of this assessment is, also, available online as an application at www.davidbsavage.com.

#	Aspect	Rank	Remarks/ Recommendations
1	We start with the end in mind and work back to today.		
2	We have positively experienced the value of collaboration together.		
3	We understand our clients' needs.		
4	Our clients/communities actively collaborate with us.		
5	We seek out those that disagree/speak out with different ideas.		
6	We have a clearly stated set of agreed-upon principles for working together that respects the ethical values of our members.		
7	We are clear on our intention for each collaboration.		
8	We ensure a variety of perspectives are represented.		
9	We identify conflicting interests and address them.		
10	We listen and listen and listen.		
11	We have clearly established the "Why."		
12	We have the necessary resources to accomplish the objectives.		
13	We have the support of those outside our team.		
14	We have clear accountabilities for the team and each member.		
15	We have a transparent structure and reporting.		
16	We have established team work communication principles.		

17	We respect all members and "have their back."		
18	We trust one another, the team and the network.		
19	When one of us believes something is not right, we listen to them.		
20	We share information in ways that increase understanding, encourage discussion, and enhance participation in decision-making.		
21	We have appropriate education and support for that training.		
22	We have effective team processes including collaborative decision-making.		
23	We co-create a climate of shared leadership and collaborative practice.		
24	We take time to have fun at work and to maintain our collective health and individual well being.		
25	We work in a variety of places inside and outside our organization and inside and outside offices.		
26	We are aware of and take steps to identify situations that are likely to lead to disagreements or conflicts, including role ambiguity, power gradients, and differences in goals		
27	We know and understand strategies to deal with conflict.		
29	Team members have guidelines for addressing disagreements.		

30	When we hold team meetings they are purpose- driven and focussed on the end result.		
31	We spend real time with those that we are serving or working with.		
32	We ensure that when a member's involvement is not needed they are free to disengage and remain informed.		
33	We are consistently inclusive, of all team members, touching base, keeping those who may not be directly involved in "the loop."		
34	We challenge ourselves to bigger dreams.		
35	We meet our time deadlines.		
36	We meet our budgets and forecasts.		
37	We see that different people lead at different times.		
38	We are recognized and compensated with regard to how we collaborate and the success of our outcomes.		
39	We see ourselves as a strong, successful, and true team.		
40	We are highly regarded by our clients/ investors/ community.		
	Total		

With this assessment, each aspect must then be addressed and ways to improve identified. The more useful exercise beyond what the scores may indicate is to discuss openly the results with the team and ascertain where improvements and celebrations are called for. Remember this: each project, challenge, opportunity, goal may be its own unique collaboration. A member who is a constructive critic, perfectionist or introvert may be expected to generally rank your project lower than an optimist, "team player" or extrovert. The assessment is not to encourage the team to agree on the rankings; rather, insights are generated with respect to differences, trends, weaknesses and strengths of the team, project or collaboration. Like the Nine Domains reviewed later in this book, leaders are to evaluate and tend to the health of the group to better work together. The assessment is not to weed out those that differ. Those that differ are often a team's strength.

Using the assessment as you start a collaboration as well as once you complete the collaboration are equally important. When you start a collaboration, the assessment may serve as a checklist to complement the 10 Steps in this book. The goal is to continuously focus on and improve the culture of collaboration in your organization.

These assessments may be charted over time by a team, an organization and a collective that extends far outside your organizations boundaries. Revise the assessment to best suit your collaborative.

Looking at the results of the assessment:

- What becomes more evident?

- Where are the gaps?

- Can you identify your team's blind spots?

- Do you notice common themes?

- Are there wide discrepancies between the rankings of individual team members on any given question or group of questions?

- What do the results inform you about your organization's ecosystem?

Are the leaders working constantly to provide the mechanisms, alignments and resources required? Can we truly hear, let go of judgments and expectations, and see possibilities greater than our own? These are some of the questions you may choose to consider quarterly and annually to assess your progress overall in building success. This assessment of the collaborative culture in your organization is most useful when done repeatedly over time and reviewed collaboratively. The transparent and constructive review of the assessment with your team will further the collaborative nature, openness, trust and engagement of your team. Laura Humelle and I offer an even more detailed assessment tool and process for our clients.

Centre of Excellence in Collaborative Leadership

Leadership is difficult. Leadership that relies heavily on collaboration is more difficult.
Rod McKay

Hummelle and I are creating a Centre of Excellence in Collaborative Leadership to assist organizations in advancing their corporate culture and successes. The following excerpt is from an introduction to the Centre of Excellence initiative largely composed by Hummelle:

A 2014 literature review conducted by *Ahead of the Curve Consulting* found an array of opportunities for collaboration that are being seized by companies around the world. While there are many positive examples of collaborative workplace models, authors Alan MacCormack of the Harvard Business School[8] and his partners from Wipro, who examined more than 40 collaborative innovation projects, concluded that when companies apply their traditional approach to collaborative endeavors, they make three critical mistakes:

- They don't consider the strategic role of collaboration, but see it only as a tactic for reducing costs. As a result, their efforts are misaligned with their business strategy.

- They don't organize effectively for collaboration. Instead they treat partners like suppliers of parts or raw materials, and manage them using a procurement function.

- They don't make long-term investments to develop collaborative capabilities. Instead they assume their existing staff and processes can handle the challenge.

These same authors caution that:

> Most organizations are not designed for collaboration. Executives don't appreciate what collaborative working truly entails and thus assume that their existing processes, infrastructure, and management practices are suitable for collaboration. They're not. Moreover, the nature of work is changing, requiring a set of skills, behaviors, and role definitions that are quite different than those that previously brought about individual and organizational success. Peel away at the symptoms, and lack of collaborative ability gets exposed as a root cause of failure.

It is the intention that our Centre of Excellence in Collaborative Leadership and Change Management will provide the expertise to guide businesses and organizations toward an organizational design/structure that supports collaboration as well as skills, behaviors, attitudes roles, etc. that enable a collaborative organization to succeed. An example of which follows:

Step 1:   Investigate the collaborative tools for a project, initiative, business, organization or industry.

Step 2:   Draft a collaborative vision statement.

Step 3:   Run a series of workshops to identify the ways in which collaboration can help them reach their business vision.

Step 4:   Benchmark important collaboration metrics, which are necessary for assessing progress making sure to benchmark current perceptions of the value of collaboration as well as readiness.

Step 5:   Start building collaboration capabilities in each dimension of people, processes and technology with the goal of gaining some early successes and demonstrate the value of collaboration. Early wins in turn increase buy-in and tangible examples of how to implement future collaborative efforts.

Step 6: Establish test-and-learn processes that help people to be mindful that collaboration is a work in progress (Collaboration Guide: Creating a Collaborative Enterprise Cisco Systems, Inc., 2009).

A progression on collaboration is emerging: awareness, education, assessment, design, access to necessary resources and processes, and then my 10-step process (as noted later).

A collaborative that extends beyond your corporate borders, done well, will generate ideas, relationships, trust, innovation, sales and profits beyond the limitations of a single business entity. To create the environment, engagement and perception of a truly open approach, consider creating a new structure (moving forward together on economic development, tourism, education, community building and more) for collaborative that cross-connect existing silos. A Centre of Excellence may, also, be used as an external support to build collaborative outcomes within an organization. Centers of excellence are teams of people with specialized expertise who work together to develop and promote best practices in their area of responsibility. Centers of excellence may provide subject matter guidance to the rest of the enterprise, or may deliver tangible business services which, in the case of collaboration, serve to:

- Address fragmentation across organizational departments, tool sets, and vendors.

- Enhance collaboration effectiveness, realizing cost efficiencies, and keeping ahead of the curve of external pressures.

- Create a cohesive enterprise collaboration strategy in order to reduce or eliminate duplication of effort, reduce costs, and deploy a common set of tools that meet the needs of end users.

- Address collaboration requests on an enterprise-level basis versus on a case-by-case basis by using a systematic approach to optimizing the collaboration.

- Assess organizational maturity and readiness for enterprise collaboration across departments.

- Encourage a culture of collaboration across the organization to effectively implement collaboration solutions that resonate with end users, develop high uptake, and deliver concrete business value.

- Properly equip external stakeholders with the tools they need to get the job done in an age when the breadth and depth of collaboration tools is greater than ever before.

- Establish a centralized training, development and coaching program and appoint "collaboration champions" in targeted teams or business groups.

- Develop or realize the network of people and resources currently available, and

- Move area priorities that have already been identified but are not yet being championed outside specific organizations and to create success through collaboration.

Good Leaders Know
They Don't Know It All

The capacity of a leader to provide a direction, to weave that dream
of what can be, requires successful inclusion of and continual
engagement of all stakeholder groups.

Jim McCormick, past President, Progressive Conservative
Association of Alberta, Calgary, Alberta

Even more important than awareness of threats and opportunities, allies
and opponents is self-awareness.

Through my career of forty years in business and in conflict management,
one thing that I have learned is that I don't know it all and others do have
answers that can create "Ah ha!" moments. I just need to be strong enough to
not be strong and to be open enough to allow others to actually see me and
see themselves as most important.

The "busyness" of our business, the distraction of communication styles, and
modern technology really minimize the opportunity to allow what needs to come
naturally. So often in management we tend to be reactive, responding under stress
to deadlines, focusing a lot of our energy on logic, economics, science, technology,
accounting, law—all of those left brain types of things. At the end of the day, those
are so incomplete. They're important, but they're so incomplete.

Several years ago, for my clients, I designed a "To Be" note pad. We have
all seen daily "To Do" lists that help us focus on the highest priority activities/
outcomes first. The common leakage for most of us on most days is to start
addressing the little things that we can get done quickly rather than the ones
that really add value. My "To Be" note pad looked like this;

On this day, I choose:
To set this Intention:

_____

To embrace this Value:

_____

To Be these three things:

_____

_____

_____

To Do these two things:

_____

_____

Notice that when we set intention, focus on our values, how we are in this world and then our actions, our achievements grow. Our achievements grow because our relationships expand through respect, trust and belief. When we place the "Doing" above our Being and our Values, in time we will fail. Those other people who are drawn to our Doing will not be loyal if we are only "projects" without heart.

When asked what thing about humanity most surprised him, the Dalai Lama answered; "Man! He sacrifices his health to make money. Then he sacrifices money to recover health. He is so anxious about the future that he does not enjoy the present. The result being that he does not live in the present or the future. He lives as if he is never going to die and he dies never really having lived."

We can create our breakthroughs when we allow others in and allow other wisdoms to flourish. There is a great opportunity in this world to come together to deal with the challenges and not be in such a hurry; we must go slowly before we can go fast.

In leadership in particular, it's all about building rapport and understanding. There's no real point in having one-sided communications. There is power in all the people that we surround ourselves with, so let them in and allow a place for disputes, conflicts, and diverse opinions—let in those people that you don't easily get along with all the time. Their perspectives can be very valuable resources to management and leaders. They're so valuable because people wouldn't fight us or be positional toward our cause unless there was a basic underlying value or interest that we hadn't yet seen. Once we spend time honoring and respecting their diverse opinions and their different perceptions, we can get a better understanding and perhaps shift our own perception so that we can all move forward.

> In the collaborative leadership model, a collaborative leader facilitates dialog ensuring all voices are heard and counted. A collaborative leader considers the past, the present and the future, allowing space for dialog to consider where we've been, where we are now and where we wish to go. A collaborative leader clarifies assumptions knowing that it is misunderstandings that derail the process. Collaborative leaders must be both humble and courageous. Humble because they know that they alone do not have all the answers. Courageous because they must trust that it takes the knowledge of many to create meaningful and sustainable results. They work toward consensus knowing that any solution will fail unless there is agreement between all. For collaboration to work, people must be accountable and responsible to the collaborative process. Doing what they say and saying what they do while acting with integrity. This process takes time but the results are amazing and well worth the investment!
>
> —*Denise Chartrand*

To be the leader, you must see yourself as leader and stand for what's most important to you before you can expect others to acknowledge your vision. Today's definition of leadership is very different from what we've traditionally felt. Leadership used to be the people with the authority got to tell others what to do. There are many people with authority who are not leaders because they haven't yet made the connection and found out what's most important.

When some of my clients in the oil and gas industry have trouble with communities, with the public, with environmentalists, etc., it's often because people within the organization feel that, when they go to work, they can't be environmentalists, or they can't be the public. But we're already all of those things. We are all of those things, and that's how we need to act in organizations and as leaders.

First and foremost, leaders figure out where their center lies. They allow their intuition, artistry and creativity, and all of the aspects of who they can be, to simply exist. From that point, they allow themselves to look for the same in others. They coach people that they work with to look for the same in themselves and to speak their own truth, speak what's most important, and to hold each other truly accountable from that place of grounded values, interests and respect.

Once you get to that "realness" point with people in your organization, with those in your community, with the stakeholders of your company, etc., then everything will run much more smoothly. The bumpiness, the conflict, and the friction are gone. That leader may not agree with those stakeholders or those others, but there's respect first, so the communication is clear, and the game plan, the resistance, and the hostility are diminished.

> If all you have learned is effective behavior, then when the stakes are high and it matters most, those behaviors will fail you. We must cultivate inner or spiritual intelligence. In turbulent times, when the pace of change makes your head spin, business leaders and public servants alike want a system that helps them stay balanced as they face unprecedented complexity and uncertainty. Consensus is growing in the business community that "the next big thing" in leadership relates to transforming the capabilities of leaders themselves. Reality has leapt ahead of people's capacity to cope, no less thrive. Leaders need tools for examining how they operate, and methodologies for evolving to new mindsets and behaviors. The ability to "lead yourself" is emerging as today's new leadership requirement.
>
> —*Erica A. Fox, my co-founder of the Global Negotiation Insight Institute and author of the New York Times bestseller* Winning from Within, *Amsterdam, Netherlands.*

Knowing What Is Real and True Is Essential to Leading in a Culture of Collaboration

When we lead people who know more about what we are doing than we do, we can't just tell them what to do and how to do it. We have to ask, listen and learn.
Marshall Goldsmith, author, Rancho Santa Fe, California

What we see, what we believe, what we know...is our interpretation filtered by our experiences, information, senses and judgments. What we project as real may not be real at all. I have learned that practicing curiosity, being open to all our wisdom, embracing diversity of opinion and allowing space for those that come from a different place is a powerful way of allowing agreements to be built that may never have otherwise existed. Ask yourself: What perceptions get in the way of allowing agreements to be built by you that may never have otherwise? What assumptions are you making about the other facts or people involved? When do you wish you would have known more, acted differently, invested in a negotiation with different people? How might you further develop your awareness of your own barriers?

With higher awareness and respect for others, more and more of us are seeing the manipulations and intellectual dishonesty too often represented in the media and social media. I invite those who seek to understand and co-create to connect in any way we can for our future, our economy, our planet and our communities. Unlike never before, we now have one or two degrees of separation from the people and wisdom that will guide us. First, though, I ask myself, what I choose to invest my energy and wisdom in. It starts within.

It starts in spirit. Then it moves to seeing ourselves and others. Then courage moves us to take our path. Collect your "merits" from those who make trouble.

We have touched on awareness of threats and opportunities. We have touched on awareness of self. We must also be aware of others. And how we are in relationship with others.

> Real compassion extends to each and every sentient being, not just to friends, or family or those in terrible situations. True love and compassion extend even to those who wish to harm you. Try to imagine your enemies are purposefully making trouble in order to help you accumulate positive forces for shaping the future, what Buddhists call "merit" by facing them with patience. If your life goes along too easily, you become soft. Trying circumstances help you develop inner strength, and the courage to face difficulty without emotional breakdown. Who teaches this? Not your friend, but your enemy.[9]
>
> *Alan D. MacCormack*

Be Open to Other Perspectives

A leader [should] use his skill and ability to conduct
a fair process of discovery.
Cinnie Noble, President, Cinergy Coaching, Toronto, Ontario

When people look through a different lens than they have previously, they are stronger for it, not weaker. Openness to learning is courageous and necessary for evolution. Embracing diversity strengthens.

If we change our hearts and perceptions, we change our world from one of separation, frustration and judgment to oneness.

There are many different perspectives. I am inviting you to open yourself to a number of different and contrary perspectives and start your learning and deciding from there. We waste too much time taking positions and celebrating those that divide us. When you read or watch a communication, from a corporation, a politician, an environmental group or any ad, question it: "What are they trying to convince me of and how can I decide for myself?" To change our habits, we must first change one thing. I challenge you simply to notice when you react, sense or have certainty about anything. Simply notice. Then ask, does this belief or judgment serve my best interests today? Simply notice. What is true? What if it wasn't true? What questions might you ask? What people? Who are these people? Who has the courage and independence to challenge my beliefs?

Begin from a Point of "Not Knowing"

What is the most important reason to collaborate? To learn.
Peter K. Hisch, Superintendent of Fuels Management at BC Wildfire Service,
Cranbrook, British Colombia

Look up "not knowing" and you will find synonyms like ignorant, blank, unconscious, negligent and uninformed. But not knowing is also a strength. Not knowing allows space for others.

As Gil Fronsdale describes the concept, "Not-Knowing" is emphasized in Zen practice, where it is sometimes called "beginner's mind." An expert may know a subject deeply, yet be blinded to new possibilities by his or her preconceived ideas. In contrast, a beginner may see with fresh, unbiased eyes. The practice of beginner's mind is to cultivate an ability to meet life without preconceived ideas, interpretations, or judgments." [10]

In my life, I find "not knowing" and curiosity are the best invitations to learning. In my life, I know that together I can accomplish far more than I can alone. Certainty creates blindness to possibilities. Certainty overvalues what we believe and what we choose. Uncertainty opens us to fresh thinking and new relationships. When a CEO asks me to work with them, I start with, "How comfortable are you with not knowing the outcome?"

When faced with a sense of certainty, I ask any three questions. These questions always provide great value. There is no magic to what those three questions are. The magic is in the respect you are showing to others and their level of engagement, and the importance of clarity over assumptions.

Collaboration done well creates an abundant, healthy and sustainable future. Collaboration done badly, as is too common in organizations, often leads to frustration, failure and wasted resources.

How many business executives do you know who are also passionate about our environment? How many aboriginals do you know who are successful in business? How many environmental leaders do you know who believe in collaboration? If you don't know any, what is stopping you from including them in your network? If you do know many, how are you bringing all of them together in one circle? Collaboration is holistic. Collaboration does not separate.

Leadership is yours (not others). Collaboration is your powerful magnet. You are important. We are the answer. Collaboration is the way we create our shared future. Collaboration is also the way we support one another in crisis.

Collaboration Requires New Business Paradigms

There's a very powerful synergy that comes from a well-functioning group. I often use that example from that movie of many years ago of "Apollo 13" when they were stuck up there and they had to get these guys in a room and said, "Here's what you've got. Figure it out." They had to work together to find a solution.

Kathy Porter

As we shift from command-and-control to collaborative leadership, let's, also, change the standards that we operate under. Compare the old to the new business paradigm and consider where you fit today and where you choose to fit tomorrow.

Old Business Paradigm:

- Quarterly reports

- Short-term economics on capital projects

- Incentives paid on one-year performance, getting projects built as planned on time and on budget

- Corporate cultures that see people and resources only as inputs

- "Us" verses "them" attitudes

- I don't have time to…

- We are not responsible for…

New Business Paradigm:

- See the bigger opportunities and challenges.

- Recognize the impact on our environment, our communities and our economies long term.

- We can no longer see ourselves as separate.

- We can no longer see the impacts of our corporations as separate.

- Capture the opportunity of sustainability into how we do our business every day. These leaders and corporations will outperform those that don't. Those that don't will continue to see communities, the environment and long-term economic health as challenges.

Your Paradigms:

Are you open to change and changing your behaviors to understand:

- Why the future matters?

- What are the qualities of a collaborative leader?

- What would a leader do?

- What do you choose?

- What behavior will you change now?

As that leader, I challenge you to use the 10 Steps to create the collaborative that serves you and your dreams.

When the circle creates options and pathways, ensure that the evaluation and decision making is done in ways that honor the present and the future. Look at the ideas, concepts and projects through the lens of economic, environmental and social sustainability.

At times, a company, a leader, or a president must simply be directive— hard and fast—and hold people accountable. As companies grow, they realize that if they want to attract, retain and build the best people and the best organization, leading through the lens of economic, environmental and social sustainability is one of the best ways to attract and retain people and build the best organization. The best people don't want to work anywhere other than a place where they can learn, be valued and make a meaningful contribution to their organization. Their organization must align with the individual's values and purpose.

Engagement, and the accountability that grows out of it, occurs when we ask people to be in charge of their own experience and act on the well being of the whole. Leaders do this by naming a new context and convening people into new conversations through questions that demand personal investment. This is what triggers the choice to be accountable for those things over which we can have power, even though we may have no control. In addition to convening and naming the question, we add listening to the critical role of leadership. Listening may be the single-most powerful action the leader can take. Leaders will always be under pressure to speak, but if building social fabric is important, and sustained transformation is the goal, then listening becomes the greater service.

This kind of leadership—convening, naming the question, and listening—is restorative and produces energy rather than consumes it. It is leadership that creates accountability as it confronts people with their freedom. In this way, engagement-centered leaders bring kitchen table and street corner democracy into being.

> The research is pretty compelling to say that the longest-term solutions, the most buy in, the most commitment come when people come together and collaborate...The point is collaboration means staying open to whatever happens.
>
> *Jeanne McPherson, PH.D, McPherson Workforce*
> *Development, Kennewick, Washington*

PART THREE

The 10 Essential Steps to Collaboration

Collaboration requires a very humble posture. Recognizing that we all have something to learn in any relationship is one of the most helpful pieces when you're pulling off any collaboration.
Tara Russell, President, Fathom Cruise Lines, Boise, Idaho

We have explored the Why and the Discipline of Collaboration. Now, we move to How. There are certain essential steps to creating great outcomes that enable us to surpass our expectations of working together. Too often, leaders will decide they must collaborate and their first action is to call a meeting. In that meeting, the leader will bring together her/his most trusted employees to brain storm ideas and create action plans. Stop! Here is a far more effective system. This is a system. This is not an event. When this process becomes how you work together, your organization will evolve into the new business paradigm. This is your step-by-step guide.

THE **10** STEPS

BUILD YOUR CULTURE, LEARN TOGETHER, & CREATE BREAKTHROUGH THINKING

1
SET INTENTION
DECLARE YOUR
HONEST PURPOSE

2
BE AWARE
ENGAGE OTHERS
WITH AN
OPEN HEART

3
EMBRACE
CONFLICT
SEEK OUT THOSE
THAT SPEAK OUT

4
SEEK DIVERSITY
BRING IN MANY
PERSPECTIVES

5
DESIGN THE
COLLABORATION
IMAGINE SUCCESS
AND CREATE THE
RIGHT CONTAINER

6
COME TOGETHER
ENGAGE WITH
RESPECT
AND TRUST

7
LISTEN DEEPLY
REALIZE WHAT WANTS
TO BE HEARD BUT
IS NOT SPOKEN

8
COLLABORATE
WITH VISION
TAP INTO THE
COLLECTIVE
WISDOM.

9
NOW LEAD
WITH PURPOSE AND
ACCOUNTABILITY

10
MAKE IT SO
POSITIVELY CHANGE
THE ENERGY AND THE
FUTURE TOGETHER

Step 1: Set Intention and Declare Your Purpose

If our leaders could just focus on solving the problems instead of pointing fingers at one another and one-upmanship, I think we have so much brilliance in those people that we could actually do more good if they work together and stepped out of their ego.
Linda Matthie, Author and Joint Venture Specialist, Cabo San Lucas, Mexico

Far too often, we rush into things without stopping to ask; what is my purpose? What is my intention? Even worse, often we think we know the answer before we start. An oft-repeated dictum from an executive is, "Don't bring me a problem unless you are also bringing me the answer." What if the problem would be better understood, accepted, answered and celebrated if it was solved together?

What if we acknowledged that lone rangers often create danger?

Most every morning over the past thirty years, when I awake in the morning, before I rise I set my intention for the coming day. This is what I hope for today.

Think about how you think. How you think creates how you perceive. How you perceive creates your judgments. Your judgments create your actions. Your actions create your life. Your life creates how you think.

Even before I set my intention, I must open my mind and heart.

During our time in 2015 developing a Centre of Excellence in Collaborative Leadership and Change Management, Hummelle advised, "We must appreciate the current leadership 'mind fields' that focus on command and control leadership, focus on sustaining the existing organizations and beliefs." Mind

Fields may also be mine fields. There are areas that have and will blow up our paths. If we look at collaborative leadership from the perspective of the existing hierarchies in organizations, there is an incongruency. By its very nature a Centre of Excellence in Collaborative Leadership and Change Management must be a fresh collective that focuses solely on its purpose and is neither owned nor controlled by any one of the "silos." We envision our Centre of Excellence to serve the following three pillars:

1. Leadership development including collaborative leadership and change management education and coaching to build the mind set of team and cross organizational focus,

2. The formalization of a significant collaborative network of people and resources to serve the interests of organizations and people in the East Kootenays, and

3. A committed team of professionals and organizational leaders to get things done. Taking work that individual organizations (governmental, not for profit, associations and businesses) have done and creating an effective collaboration to accomplish what the East Kootenays need most (and individuals and individual organizations struggle separately to achieve or even dream).

As leaders, we must focus less on our own organization (our own silo) and see what is possible by working together. When we create a shared vision of the future, we may then focus on how we make it happen. Those leaders and organizations that achieve this mind set/mind field, see many more possibilities than those that look only within their silos.

> Silo is a business term that has been passed around and discussed at many board room tables over the last 30 years. Unlike many other trendy management terms this is one issue that has not disappeared over the years. Departmental silos are seen as a growing pain for most organizations of all sizes. It is the duty of the executive leaders and management to prepare and equip their teams with the proper mind-set to break down this destructive organizational barrier.[11]

Think big. Think open. Think "pluralverse." [12] Think possible. Do not be constrained or prejudiced by trying to stay within the perspectives, people and resources within one department, organization, community or nation. A universe of unity and a pluralverse of diversity are the seeds of collaboration.

Be intentional. Be intentional with all you do. Before you start a conversation or a collaboration or "tweet," set your intention.

When you are present, take your time, pay special attention to the other, explore and enjoy. Collaboration is fantastic. When you rush in with only your own needs and desires in mind, not considering the impact on others, very often you finish not very satisfied, wishing there was more to it or worse.

Collaboration is a journey, a relationship, a discovery. Collaboration is a way of being in this world.

"If you want to go fast, go alone. If you want to go far, go together." African proverb

A Touchstone for Every Turning

When we embark on a journey, clarifying intent is our crucial first step. Knowing what we want and establishing a clear, conscious aim opens the door for all that will follow and continually orients us on the path. It becomes a touchstone for every turning. We must have a pure, honest, and warm-hearted motivation, and on top of that, determination, optimism, hope, and the ability not to be discouraged. The whole of humanity depends on this motivation.

His Holiness, the Dalai Lama. (Lama, 2011)

Take a moment and ponder this: "The whole of humanity depends on…"

My parents built a beautiful family cabin in a mountain valley in southern British Columbia with the name Tulameen. As a family we spent many happy times at Tulameen with cousins, aunts, uncles and fast friends. Tulameen has been our family touchstone. When Mom and Dad died in 2001, they willed their cabin to the five of us adult children; Carol, Bill, Bob, Sylvia and I. While experts and friends warned us "family cabins never work," we wanted to welcome current and future generations to Mom and Dad's family gathering place. This place is sacred to our family. Tulameen is adventure, nature, love and family. Sacred can be difficult.

Each spring, the five of us enjoy a long May weekend at the cabin doing the maintenance required and reconnecting from our busy lives. Each fall, we meet at Tulameen again to conduct our business meeting for the year. Adult sisters and brothers with families and lives of their own have many interests, challenges, opportunities and hopes. At times, these clash over what to do about Tulameen. Assumptions are made, judgments follow and preconceived solutions are not far behind. To clear the energy and the conversation, each year we begin our annual general meeting by setting our intention. "We are here by the grace of Mom and Dad. Let their intentions for this place guide us today." This sounds like a religious preamble. And this saves us from ourselves every year. We let the intention of our parents in our hearts while we decide on the business and the future of Tulameen. The solutions we came with are left with our shoes on the front porch outside. The outcomes we create together are in service of our parents' dream.

If there is one single step that can change how we are together and allow us to release our busy-ness this is the one. Slow down, breathe and be here now. Find the breathing space. Leave the "to do" place. Set intention.

The Role of Empathy in Negotiation

There were many dialogues which were unblocked by the entrance of empathy.

Tina Spiegel.

Earlier we explored the value of mindfulness and curiosity for leaders. When we are present with others and open to what is in this moment, we have the opportunity to connect better with others. Add empathy as a leader, as a negotiator and as a collaborator, and you will find greater understanding and potential.

During 2010, 2011 and early 2012, I videotaped over a hundred people from five countries on their wisdom on negotiation. The one hundred people who shared their advice on collaboration for this book are almost entirely a different group. A brief compilation of a few of those interviews are on my website: http://www.davidbsavage.com/resources/

From those video interviews, here are observations from two accomplished women in very different fields:

Brenda Kenny is President of the Canadian Energy Pipeline Association, which represents large oil and natural gas pipelines in Canada and the United States.

David: Brenda, in this moment, name one quality of a master negotiator.

Brenda: That's a big question but the one that comes to mind for me is empathy. I think what's really critical more so now than ever before is an ability to really understand where each side is coming from. Many of the issues that we're coping with and negotiating around are very complex and very heartfelt. It's not enough just to quantify things and try to move to a middle space; you really have to understand where the other person is coming from.

Margaret Wheatley has published many books from 1992's *Leadership and the New Science* to 2014's *How Does Raven Know? Entering Sacred World/A Meditative Memoir.*[13] Wheatley writes and teaches around the world on issues of community, non-hierarchical leadership, an orderly universe, spirituality and the role that women are playing as they step forward to lead.

David: Margaret, in this moment, name one quality of a master negotiator.

Margaret: The word that comes instantly to mind is the one quality is empathy. That if we are able to put ourselves in the shoes of the person we are negotiating with and develop some sense of connection so that we're not opposites opposing each other, I find this is extremely powerful to get in the mind and heart and aspirations of someone who feels like they are an opponent until the moment I ask them what their aspiration is here.

Two very different women both in positions of great international influence and they both tell us that empathy is a quality of a master negotiator. Empathy is their starting place; not power, control, economics—but empathy. Throughout the entire one hundred plus interviews, most all, men and women, Americans, Dutch, British, French, Canadians and South Africans, spoke of the importance to connect with and understand the other side.

As we start, and even as we are planning to collaborate, let's speak to our intentions and qualities as we prepare for and engage in collaboration. How will we "be" and who do I choose to "be" in this collaboration? What is your aspiration?

Defining the Question in the Context of Healthcare

Will health care in 2025 look little like health care today. It's time to look at the what, where, how, when, why and who in new ways.

David Savage

Einstein is believed to have said that given an hour to answer a question, he recommends spending the first 55 minutes defining the question. Asking the real and best question saves us from wasting resources on the superfluous. Before we go down rabbit holes, let's spend far more time exploring what the real question is.

Today, ensuring effective and practical health care is a major challenge to people and governments around the world. I serve as a facilitator and consultant helping primary health care professionals to come together and to find solutions. As I write this book, one of my great clients is the Divisions of Family Practice in British Columbia. Our goals are: 1) to confirm and strengthen the family doctor and patient continuous relationship including better support for the needs of vulnerable patients, 2) to enable patients that want a family doctor to find one and 3) to increase the capacity of the primary health care system.

As populations age and as the strain on health care systems grows, we look for more ways to change the way we connect and deliver health care. Yes, the obvious solution is "hire more doctors!" But that solution is proving impractical. There are a limited number of doctors, they are in great demand everywhere and the governments, service providers, employers, people and others that are paying for health care are pretty tapped out already. In addition, family doctors are feeling increased pressure that comes from lack of funding, long hours, increased liability, and more "at risk" or "high needs" patients. Family doctors are also aging and do not wish to continue a 60-plus-hour workweek.

With the Divisions of Family Practice, we started with the focus on getting all residents "matched" to a family doctor. Then we started asking different questions such as: "What if the solution involved having fewer (or no increase in) family doctors?" Through our collaborative effort over a seven- month period, we worked with family doctors and many other primary health care professionals and support organizations in four communities in south-eastern BC. Three main themes arose as we searched for unique problem sets and opportunities with a diverse group of people:

1. In every community or city, the primary health care providers (general practitioners, nurses, nurse practitioners, pharmacists, health food sellers, addiction counselors, psychologists, chiropractors, practice coaches and more) did not know who was doing this work in their area. The chair of the Hospital Board stated, "I had no idea you were all here." The disconnection and lack of a sense of, or actual, primary health care community was a surprise.

2. Each community, or city, has its unique relationships, challenges and opportunities. The town of Kimberley, British Columbia is a 20-minute drive from Cranbrook, which is an hour's drive from Creston and Fernie (opposite directions). Yet all four communities worked with their own circumstances and skills and came up with their own unique recommendations and action plans to deal with the challenges faced in health care. There is no cookie-cutter solution; each group experiences the challenges differently and worked to develop their own priorities.

3. We realized that a key solution to the problem "too many people do not have a family doctor" is impacting how primary health care providers, especially family doctors, work together and where they connect with the patient. The old system, medical and financial, saw the family doctor as the center of the health care wheel. New thinking coming from groups across the world, and the healthcare system in British Columbia looks to develop a stronger health care team by conducting triage early and inserting nurses, paramedics and other professionals and assistants to provide the support for doctors and patients. The doctor need not be the first point of contact nor the one that all the specialists download their work to.

There are many innovative ideas that the Divisions of Family Practitioners are working through, and few of them were expected at the start. Through bringing the right people together, working as a team focused on the same problem with different perspectives and being open to "tearing up the rule book" and looking at what our real work is then finding the most effective ways to perform it for our stakeholders (the public), there is a sense of possibility. The woman that I directly serve on this initiative is Jo Ann Lamb, Primary Care Coordinator and GP for Me Lead, East Kootenay Division of Family Practice, Kimberley, British Columbia. Lamb has a successful and respected career in health care and management. The tag line on her email is "Dwell in Possibility!"

The possibilities that are being developed in Canada and across the world are focused on better service by health care teams, by focusing on preventative health care and education, by increased access to useful information and increased accountability by patients. We have vast resources and intelligence that is relatively unproductive to date. Health care in 2025 will look little like health care today. It's time to look at the what, where, how, when, why and who in new ways.

The critical question is, why are there so many unattached patients? You get into a very different conversation if you ask, "What is the best way we can provide primary health care to patients?" Do you see in this example how funding and pressure from the public may lead you to asking the wrong question? If we decided together to completely re-engineer the primary health care system in your state, province, nation or community, where might we start? We may start with asking what are the most important values, characteristics and measurables of a great primary health care system? Now that can start us toward breakthrough collaboration!

Step 2: Be Aware of Adversarial Agendas and Engage with an Open Heart

When Collaborative Dispute Resolution fails, it is typically because
of the concealed undisclosed issues of the parties involved.
Ronald Melin Supancic, Owner of The Law Collaborative,
Los Angeles, California

Before you begin, be aware of the values, interests, personalities and perspectives that you will want to include. Also, be aware of the people that will fight to defeat you. Just because a group of people appear to be working for the good of the community, doesn't mean everyone in the community will support and engage in the collaboration. Self-interest most often trumps public interest. As Supancic writes:

Sadly, I have been a part of a number of cases in which the parties engaged with secret agendas that involved a refusal to be truthful, to disclose facts, and the withholding of vital information, which inevitably caused the collaboration to fail. There is no room for dishonesty in the Collaborative Process. That is the bottom line. Attorneys who claim to be collaborative but continue to bring their adversarial habits, skills, tactics, and techniques to the table, are equally responsible. I have seen collaborations fail because of an attorney who cannot give up the idea of winning at any cost and who clings to adversarial vocabulary and tactics.

Make Certain Their Heads Hang Down When They Leave

Creativity, technology, social change and globalization have created the opportunity to rethink how we organize and come together.[14]

A business friend asks me to meet her, urgently. "Hillary" wants to tell me something important and asked for my ear. When we meet at a small café across from her downtown Calgary office tower, she lets me know that she is nearing completion of her Master's in Leadership from a respected university. She is so tired of not having influence in her work even though she is part of the management team. Hillary is looking for coaching from me on her next steps in a leadership role outside of the multinational corporation that pays her today. She is considering consulting to other companies. I challenge her that doing leadership work is most important from the inside of organizations. That is where the tough work is and where the breakthroughs happen. Consultants really have limited real impact on the organizations they serve working part time from the outside.

I question Hillary as to what she is experiencing. The answers she gives me are far too common: her "boss" is too busy to lead; he uses meetings simply to gather information to report up the food chain to people on higher floors and in corner offices. There is little collaboration. There is manipulation. A fellow manager, Hillary states, is constantly cranky, hostile and antagonistic. She calls him "the Grinder." When things are not going well for the corporation, the Grinder, with active encouragement from the "Boss" dumps on management, staff and every company they do business with. The past week's management meeting is but one example of how toxic the company is. They will not hit their production targets and costs are above budget. A major billion-dollar development project is under great stress and scrutiny. A meeting with the major project contractors, consultants and suppliers is set. The Grinder and the Boss demand, "Hit them hard. Show those bastards. They need to fix this now. Make certain their heads hang down when the leave the meeting." Hillary counters with "They are our partners in this project. They are the ones that actually do the work on the site. I believe that if we hammer them, they will find ways to do more of the same to us." David, my management team has no idea about leadership. Where can I go?"

I suggested that she "go inside to see you as the leader." I ask permission to do five minutes of compressed coaching for her. She says, yes, please. We explore the perspectives of this drama and these relationship challenges from three different metaphorical rooms. Hillary moves through each one and gives each one a name. I then ask her to consider given more than one perspective, more than one view of the hard-ass approach of her team leaders, what has she learned and what will she do now? She has gone inside the Grinder and the Boss's offices. Hillary accepts my challenge that she will have a new conversation with the Grinder that very afternoon.

Ninety minutes after we met, I received this email from Hillary. The header is "The magic of a conversation." The email reads, "Thanks for inspiring me for a better conversation with my colleague. You know, the conversation was different; it was deep, it was fun and it had a lot of questions - going back and forth - which achieved addressing some key points that needed to be hashed out. We got to where we needed to go. I do feel like it was a turning point. So how did I show up differently? I just approached the conversation with more heart than head. It was great to have a conversation with this person from my feminine side—I have always felt that I had to meet him in the masculine sphere—but today I learned something new. Isn't that the best thing about learning—it never stops when we open our mind to consider new possibilities. It was a great opportunity to expand the universe instead of making it small...Thank you for the coaching conversation—not what I intended when I decided that it was time to connect with you today...but as you said, things unfold the way they need to..." Faced with corporate bullying, Hillary set her intention as a collaborative leader. She had empathy for the other manager. They had a better conversation.

The dominant aggressive alpha male leader, at times, destroys value and relationships for his company's shareholders. Negotiating on behalf of an oil and gas client, I dealt with Hillary's alpha male. The situation was that my client had drilled a number of oil wells and was producing them to the alpha male company's production facilities. The produced emulsion from my client's wells is 95 percent water and 5 percent marketable oil. The costs related to the separation and reinjection of the water back into the producing formation made the production uneconomic. My client's objective was to reduce the fees charged by the facility owner to a level that would allow my client and the facility owner to make money. Over a ten-month period, I thought we had agreement. The facility owner failed to document or sign the documents I had prepared to evidence the understanding. My client kept asking for the agreements to be signed and the proper invoices to be prepared. Without those, my client couldn't pay the facility owner. After ten months of this, the facility owner finally paid attention and demanded immediate payment. I attended a meeting where five representatives of the facility owner and I tried to work this out. While we did succeed in resolving the billings and terms, my client was clear throughout that their oil wells were uneconomic and would be shut down given the facility owner's position. This is a case where the alpha male "won", my client shut down their oil wells and several millions of dollars were lost from the facility owner's net present value. They defended their fees and, in the process, lost revenue. In a production facility, less volume going through makes the costs per unit increase for the remaining volumes. My client worked hard to get the alpha male to understand the economic losses that would result from his "win." He simply went on to other priorities. My client will be building its own oil production facility in the area.

Engagement and Trust

We need each other to get things done that we can't do alone, as with a string quartet.[15]

At the December 2010 Canadian Association of Petroleum Landmen (an association of oil industry professional negotiators that I have been a member of since 1976) meeting, I asked a few key questions to a number of long-term friends who are also very experienced negotiators. I share these with you as they reflect how we are as negotiators in relationship with our peers.

> Question #1:
> *From your experience as a negotiator, given the need to share a great, confidential and complex opportunity, how many Landmen would you trust completely to negotiate for a mutual big win? My emphasis was on "trust completely." For example, you had to travel and trust the other Landmen to make the deal that benefits both your companies.*

Their answers ranged from five to 100 Landmen. Personally, my answer was about 30 that I would be prepared to give them all the information and trust them to create a great deal for me as well as them. What would your answer be? Is a negotiator who answers "none" less trusting than one who answers "one hundred"? Or is the first negotiator simply more experienced?

Would it be naive to trust completely? Or are those business relationships more reflective of the "handshake" era of the past?

Question #2:
How many negotiators, no matter how big the potential outcome for your company, would you refuse to call because of the way they dealt with you in the past?

This question was meant to be the opposite of the first one. The answers I received ranged from two to 30 negotiators that could not be trusted. Is the much lower range a positive reflection on our business relationships, ethics and professional approaches? I think so. My answer was two, and neither of those two are C.A.P.L. members or even Canadian. In my judgment, they both were hard-ass, positional and opportunistic negotiators from the U.S.A. Neither were American Association of Petroleum Landmen members. My two "never agains" arose in 1981 (Mississippi offshore) and 1998 (Massachusetts). On both occasions, I was negotiating in an environment unfamiliar to me with people unfamiliar to me. Both felt my company was in a weak position and tried their best to take advantage of us. While I am a strong advocate of interest-based negotiation and appropriate dispute resolution (ADR), I know that with some companies/individuals, I have to find a bigger stick to threaten them with (often litigation). Once they understand that the power imbalance may turn against them, they will then come back to the table. And I will not trust them.

Now a third question:
How many lists are you on?

This is the most important question. How many negotiators would include you in their list of negotiators they trust completely? How many would include you on their "never again" list?

This is the most important question of all as it is the one that reflects our reputation, relationships and success in the eyes of others. If you are on list of "trust completely" and on not one "never again" list you will have a great and long career. If you are seen as the opposite, you are likely not working as a negotiator anymore.

A major distinction for negotiators in the upstream Canadian oil and gas industry (versus other businesses or nations) is that all-in-all we are a small community that deals with one another many times during our careers. Those who make hard very one-sided deals (or are pushed by their company to) will find that their company can clean up its reputation by terminating the "bad" negotiator and hiring a "good" one. Those Landmen, and others, who act for better outcomes for all will find their negotiations far more effective and efficient than others. Is this true of you?

Look to the past to see that the "word is his bond/handshake deals" world has changed. We deal with more and more detailed formal agreements to reduce the future conflicts. A better way is to build and sustain great, trusting, honorable business relationships with fellow negotiators, stakeholders, communities and regulators. No agreement, no matter how detailed and extensive will cover every possible eventuality. A positive, respectful, trusting relationship will allow the parties to resolve problems if and when they arise. Good written agreements are very important; good working constructive, collaborative, respectful business relationships are even better.

Reflect for a moment on one of the great Canadians, Harley Hotchkiss. Those who do not know Harley can read his biography "Hat Trick" to appreciate his honor and spirit. As but one example, when the National Hockey League Board of Governors shut down the league for a season. After many months of acrimony, it was Hotchkiss (Calgary Flames owner and chair of the NHL Board of Governors) called upon Trevor Linden (head player representative of the NHL Players' Association and Vancouver Canucks captain). They met at Chicago's O'Hare airport. Through intention "to get this thing fixed, we must first start with honesty and trust." You will understand that no matter what the challenge, men like Harley Hotchkiss took the high road and built lifelong friendships with most everyone he negotiated with. Trevor Linden took the high road, as well, and is now the President of Hockey Operations for the Vancouver Canucks.

As a third-generation Calgarian and fifth-generation Canadian, I am proud that my father, Alexander Gordon Savage was described as "straight as an arrow." And, in these times where people in the oil business are increasingly labeled as "the bad guys," people in business and especially the petroleum industry must continue to build our skills, awareness and business relationships to get the very best for ourselves, our organizations, our communities, our nation and our world. We must be "straight as an arrow", trustworthy and open.

If a person's word "is as good as their bond," what is your bond worth? How many peer lists are you on? Which list? And how do you choose to negotiate? How do you choose to lead? Is your "word" valued?

Our Crisis, Their Indifference

The business world must resist the temptation to avoid collaboration, and even conflict.

Pierre Alvarez, former President of the Canadian Association of Petroleum Producers.

In the early 1990s I served as chief operating officer of Westar Petroleum, which was part of the Westar Group that also included mining, timber and the deep-sea port at Tsawwassen, south of Vancouver, BC. Westar Mining was predominately a miner of metallurgical coal for export to Japan. In the 1970s and 1980s Japanese corporations such as Mitsubishi invested heavily in metallurgical coal properties around the world. Having your major purchaser as a significant stakeholder/shareholder in your company is believed to be a strategic advantage as interests can be more closely aligned (between producer, investor and consumer). However, this alliance also can become a threat. Once the investor/consumer has significant control of your company and your competitors, it therefore has significant power over your product pricing and demand.

During the 1980s and early 1990s the price of metallurgical coal rose and fell. Westar mining had to find a way to control costs in the downturns and was prepared to share profits when prices were better than expected. The Japanese had significant downward influence on prices as they had a number of mines they could play against one another.

Westar's older Balmer Mine was unionized with the United Steelworkers of America. When Westar opened the Greenhills Mine, a Workers' Association was formed. The "deal" was that the employees at Greenhills would share some of the upside and the downside with the employer and a more progressive relationship could evolve. The United Steelworkers relationship with Westar Mining (and Kaiser Coal before them) was adversarial old style union verses management.

Westar Group had me bring our Westar Petroleum employees to the Mining operations. Overall, the benefit was to build awareness of one another's challenges, opportunities and techniques. Our intention was to link the people at Mining and Petroleum so we could each consider what worked and didn't for each division. Our Calgary-based office staff and Kindersley, Saskatchewan-based oilfield operations staff found their peers at Greenhills interesting and we could learn from one another better practices and operating efficiencies. We found no such possibility with the union employees (or at least their representatives) at the Balmer Mine. The United Steelworkers' approach to cost and productivity challenges, however, was that "we take care of our members and no one else." More progressive union leaders and representatives understand that the worker can do far better when there is a healthy partnership with management. When Westar Mining was in financial trouble, the union message was "we don't have to do anything to help the company. If Westar fails, there will be another company to employ us." There was no interest in collaboration. The Union saw Westar as simply the current boss to fight.

Regardless of the corporate and personal commitment by leaders like then Westar Mining President Peter Dolezal, the early 1990s rock bottom metallurgical coal prices and Westar Mining's mountain of debt (including that from opening up the Greenhills Mine) resulted in placing the company into bankruptcy. Much was lost. And the union is now dealing with yet another corporation struggling with yet another down cycle in the coal market. Was the union right? Or were the attempts to better align interests between workers and shareholders right?

"Right" is an elusive and perhaps impossible concept.

There are times when you just have to accept the other side will block you in every way. Those are the times when a strong leader must take definitive action and minimize her/his attempt to collaborate. When you realize the other side is not willing to collaborate, then collaboration must be set aside until the conditions are right. Creating those conditions, at times, means taking a hard line with the other organization and identifying where you have real and/or perceived leverage. In my negotiations with the hardliners and corporate bullies, I find that when I find a bigger stick, they will finally come to negotiate. In the Westar case, the old style union was closed to any collaboration. Westar Mining was lost. The Workers Association lost. And the ups and downs of the international price of metallurgical coal continues to provide huge challenges and opportunities to all involved.

In business, too often, we see "us" and "them." Even our meeting rooms are rectangles with long sides where people look at each other with separation and barriers. What if we banned those barriers and sides? Optimally, our meetings should be circles without barriers. A circle of chairs with no table in between us, immediately brings people in conflict closer to understanding "them." Imagine a campfire with a talking stick being passed around so everyone has a place and a voice.

Imagine, ensuring you have all the voices in your circle. All the voices that speak for different perspectives, cultures, professions and experiences.

The Enneagram is one way to hear all the voices and learn to speak to each member in the way that brings them into the collaboration.

The Enneagram as Insight

We are relational beings and all things flow from relationship.

Tina Spiegel.

The Enneagram is first believed to have made its appearance more than two thousand years ago in Egypt, Persia, Spain and the Middle East. Unlike the more widely known personality assessments, the Enneagram invites us to un-type ourselves and connect with others in a more meaningful and productive manner. The Golden Rule we were taught in our youth is: "Treat others the way you wish to be treated." Or in Biblical language, "Do unto others as you would have them do unto you." The Platinum Rule is far more effective in relationships; "Treat others the way they want to be treated." Makes great sense to be with others in their way rather than expect them to be like us. The Enneagram informs me of several very important things:

A) What are my tendencies and needs in relationship?

B) What are my tendencies in conflict?

C) What are the tendencies and needs of the other in this relationship?

D) What are their tendencies in conflict?

E) What are their and my underlying fears?

F) What language and behaviors light them up or shut them down?

G) How do I get more of what I want?

When I have a stronger sense of these, then I can connect, communicate and act in ways the other person understands and prefers. Whether in communication, negotiation, mediation or collaboration, "be with" the other first is most always more effective than waiting for them to come to you. Being with them builds connection, respect and trust.

In collaboration, awareness of the people you choose to engage is critical. The Enneagram also guides us to inviting the appropriate mix of personalities and styles into our collective. Below is a graphic that I developed to illustrate the strengths of the nine types as negotiators. Each type has its strengths and weaknesses. To bring the balanced mix together gives a far better, broader and more balanced perspective. Conversely, the right mix reduces the risk of tunnel vision and groupthink.

Each of the nine types has its own tendencies, focus and reactions under stress; is your main tendency toward perfection, connection, achieving, artistry, knowledge, loyalty, enthusiasm, leadership or balance? Are you more a logical, feeling or instinctive leader? There is so much to learn about ourselves and so much more to learn about the way others in our teams, clients, customers and communities react best to us.

Looking at the graphic, is there any one of the nine tendencies/types that you would consciously choose to exclude from your collaborative initiative?

With *Break Through to Yes: Unlocking the Possible within a Culture of Collaboration*, the 10 Essential Steps to Collaboration encourage you to include the nine types to the extent you are aware and have that balance available to you in your organization or network.

How might a "perfectionist/competency" centered person be in collaboration with one centered on "positive outlook/mentoring"? If your collaborative management team is led by a positive outlook type they, also, better have individuals with a strong focus on doing things right. Many organizations are led by people with Achievers and Leaders. Without a balance of types, expertise and backgrounds, collaboration will suffer.

Considering all nine types, which do you believe are missing in your organization or your collaboration style?

Possibilities with Nine Domains

Collaborative leadership revolves around the relational demands of work, particularly in environments of uncertainty.
Jeanne McPherson, Ph.D

For organizations, I am certified in and recommend the Nine Domains Approach.[16] "The Nine Domains are the nine essential components of complex systems, be they natural or designed by humans. When each of the Nine Domains is present AND they are in balance, the entire system thrives. Domains can, however, be missing or distorted. Such imbalances not only diminish the performance of a system, but may also threaten its survival. Furthermore, the Nine Domains are a new way of talking about a complete whole with interrelated parts. As such, they are a 'check list for completeness' (as stated by Don Riso, founder of the Enneagram Institute) and can be applied to the development of a team, the analysis of a particular problem, or the evaluation of an entire complex situation or crisis."

Each organization performs in a band of nine levels of functioning. Most organizations tested around the world operate in the mid ranges of performance; interpersonal control moving up to role identification moving up to mature contribution and on. Management teams often over estimate their team's level of functioning. How much does your organization stay in "interpersonal control" where the participants spend a good part of their days focusing on their authority and status? Think about a bucket of crabs. Every time a crab starts to climb out, another pulls it back down in the bucket. With better performing teams, the focus on "role identification," which means "who are we, how do we work together, what is my job? At a higher level of performance or "mature contribution," the team embraces challenge from within (but more on this later).

Are you getting the sense that collaborating successfully is difficult and complex? Great, you understand. Collaborative management must take time to build levels of trust between themselves and the executive, build their skills, and be conscious and accountable. Collaboration isn't something your organization can excel at by doing it occasionally and without a structure.

Anthony Williams and Dan Tapscott, who wrote *Radical Openness: Four Unexpected Principles for Success* suggest, "Collaborative innovation is not about a bunch of people sitting in a room constantly brainstorming with no time to reflect, nor is it about designing by committee. It's about tapping a broader talent pool and bringing together the complementary skills and knowledge required to create a superior product or solve a problem." [17]

My friend and coach, Michael Rochelle, President and CEO, MDR Strategies, LLC, Washington, D.C. has told me, "No vanguard exists for its own purposes, but exists to serve the grander purpose of the main element(s) from which it springs. The story of Moses is the story of a vanguard. The fact that he was not permitted to cross over into the Promised Land after leading the Israelites out of Egypt for 40 years is because, in anger and frustration with those he led, he lost sight of his main purpose. Consequently, he was denied the privilege of entering the Promised Land." When our own ego becomes immersed with success of our endeavors. We are simply the catalysts. Our endeavors serve that grander purpose. Our anger and frustration will separate us from the endeavor itself."

Step 3: Embrace Conflict: Seek Out Those That Speak Out

> To collaborate is to cooperate traitorously with an enemy.
> *Colin Campbell.*

Those Who Stand Against

Those who disagree have much to teach us. The value of conflict is to gain understanding, trust and build relationship. I embrace conflict because underneath there are real interests and real values that must be understood not bypassed. I would far rather work with people in conflict than people who are unengaged and passive aggressive. Those that stand up for something honor us all. In *Difficult Conversations: How to Discuss What Matters Most*, Douglas Stone, Bruce Patton and Sheila Heen share:

> In difficult conversations, too often we trade only conclusions back and forth, without stepping down to where most of the real action is: the information and interpretations that lead each of us to see the world as we do. [18]

In the summer of 2007 at the Omega Institute in upstate New York, our Global Negotiation Insight Institute welcomed forty people from around the world to hear from our thought leader Erica Ariel Fox. The focus was on negotiation and conflict resolution. Six years later, Erica published her bestseller *Winning from Within*. [19]

At our weeklong Omega retreat, we had a reasonable knowledge of the backgrounds of all the participants and their expectations. Through the second day, one woman (let's call her Gabrielle, a participant with a very challenging life background who attended many workshops in search of some breakthrough awareness or new tool) was becoming increasingly agitated but not sharing the source of her frustration. Her body language screamed anger and frustration. Most of us as leaders may have ignored the negative energy and dealt with her later to honor the group and keep the focus on the program for all. Some of us would have asked her to calm down and then invite her to talk with us after the group session is complete. Instead, Erica chose to invite Gabrielle to speak. She refused and Erica again, with love, invited her to share. While Gabrielle was speaking she became increasingly emotional. When the woman finished, Erica asked, "And, what else?" The woman was surprised and then let her perspectives and frustrations boil over. Rather than getting annoyed or defensive or angry, Erica thanked Gabrielle, summarized what she had heard and asked if that was accurate. Great leaders and facilitators will stop there. However, Erica then turned to the group of forty and asked, "Is there any part of what Gabrielle shared that you agree with? Really, this isn't about being nice. Let's find what we must change to include all of us," she asked again.

Nervously, a couple people put up their hands. Erica asked what part of Gabrielle's frustration were they, too, feeling? Erica heard a few comments. Most of us were uncomfortable yet curious as to what was happening. Erica again asked the group, "Is there any part of what Gabrielle has shared that you agree with?" At least a third of the group put up their hands. I could sense the energy of the group grow very positive and connected. We have honored diversity and conflict and learned something about changing the way we presented and hosted. And, equally important, Gabrielle moved from being an angry outsider to an integral active part of the group. She told us that in all her years of searching, this was the group that opened ourselves to her. Erica showed us that there is a piece of the conflict that we all share. Erica embraced conflict.

Too often, leaders avoid conflict, give in, get reactionary or waste resources focusing on being right, punishing or paying off those who oppose. Such leaders provide an incentive to be a dysfunctional team. They create teams that are just like them (homogeneous, groupthink, yes men). Around the world, the best performing teams have one thing in common, they embrace conflict, hate "groupthink" and seek out those who disagree and/or challenge the team.

Avoiding conflict is a major mistake. Conflict is positive in many ways. It indicates that the organization employs and supports people who speak up for what is most important—their values and those of their communities and stakeholders. A high-functioning team or organization finds their wisdom through adversarial perspectives. A high-performing organization also embraces all personality strengths and styles. The different perspectives allow the organization to experience the responses and outcomes internally before the proposal or plan goes out the door. Leaders who embrace diverse perspectives and challengers from within will find their culture dynamic, agile and successful. Consider this from Pierre Alverez:

> In a world where technologies such as smart phones, email and the Cloud make working alone, isolated by both distance and time so attractive. The need for collaboration has never been greater. The business world, and oil and gas in particular due to the almost endless list of lives that it affects, must resist the temptation to use these tools as ways to avoid collaboration, and even conflict. Saying I sent an email is just not good enough. Rather business should use these tools to generate more effort and enthusiasm to work together with all stakeholders to resolve issues before they reach the confrontational stage.

The Outsider

My work in leadership has been, especially with women, to encourage women to listen to their own voice, to make choices that are best for them, their families, their communities, and to hold leadership roles in simple, small ways at work and at home and in the community.

Joan Goldsmith, Author and Organizational Development Expert,
Santa Monica, California.

Several years ago, a large group of us from many nations, including South Africa, Norway, Australia, England, Canada and the United States, convened at Don Riso's big beautiful old red "Barn" at the Enneagram Institute[20] at Stone Ridge in upstate New York. We had come for an eight-day retreat to learn the Nine Domains Approach. Throughout the retreat, I felt like an outsider. When participants talked about what the usefulness of the Nine

Domains was for client organizations, I kept saying, "No, that's not it for me." As we neared the end of these intense 14-hour days, I finally spoke my perspective using different words than I had previously. Immediately the others looked at me and said, yes, I get it now, you are right. And the way we spoke of the Nine Domains was changed. For me, it was important to honor my sense and kept trying to verbalize my opposition in a way the others would hear. For the others, they listened even though I was the odd man out. In the end, we all benefitted. And that, interestingly, in the Nine Domains Approach, is the sign of a high-functioning team; the "mature contribution" level encourages members to dissent and to challenge until we finally get it right.

A highly functioning team is one where constructive criticism, push backs, challenges and diverse opinions are highly valued, encouraged and used to build better outcomes. A high-functioning team rarely says, "Yes, Sir" with conflict avoiders. A key role for me as I work within organizations is to "incite insurgency" (as one executive described me). I work to reenergize participants to challenge themselves, their teams and their organizations in ways not often seen. I poke and prod to get the team to respond. Progress is made as team members move from comfort to deep review to challenge to reflection to new insights and then to better and more sustainable deals and strategies.

In 2008, I met Bill Ury at an Association for Conflict Resolution Conference in Phoenix. As a co-author (with Rodger Fisher) of *Getting to Yes* and *Getting Past No*, Ury is widely regarded as the world's thought leader for negotiation and has been doing so for 35 years. As Ury explained, he realized that the great success in his family, at Harvard, as a negotiator on behalf of the United States and as a businessman, came largely from saying *no*. In the *Power of a Positive No* [21], he writes; "You are asserting your value. It could be your value as a human being, in a commercial context, of your product or service or brand, it could be your ethical and moral values. Ultimately you are saying *yes* to what truly matters. You are setting a clear limit, drawing a clear line, and creating a firm boundary." Say *no* more often if you care about the relationship; counter propose with something that also benefits you.

In the six-month Negotiation Mastery Circles that I lead for clients, I start with the *Power of a Positive No*. Saying no is uncomfortable and unfamiliar to most participants. I challenge you to say no most often for the next week. *No* is a clear boundary that protects what is most important to us. When you do say *yes*, it actually means *yes*.

The outsider, the brave and those who value humanity are called to speak up when so many stay silent. Seek out those who speak out.

> When the Nazis came for the communists,
> I remained silent;
> I was not a communist.
> When they locked up the social democrats,
> I remained silent;
> I was not a social democrat.
> When they came for the trade unionists,
> I did not speak out;
> I was not a trade unionist.
> When they came for the Jews,
> I remained silent;
> I wasn't a Jew.
> When they came for me,
> There was no one left to speak out.
>
> *Martin Niemöller*[22]

In the past few years, my clients and colleagues in large Canadian corporations increasingly tell me stories about the decline of independent leadership. Corporations turn increasingly to top-down commanders with technical, legal and financial Masters and Doctorates. American-controlled corporations turn increasingly to forcing American management practices and values on Canadian leaders. Chinese- and Korean-controlled corporations turn increasingly to removing all authority and independence from their Canadian executives. This is not only disgraceful and disempowering, this "take away leadership and power" trend serves to undermine the Canadians, their businesses and the nation. This trend, also, erodes the probability of innovation from those very same corporations. Change the name Canadian to American, American to Asian…and you will find similar examples. To compete and excel, we must engage, educate, empower and enthuse employees, executives and the regions in which they work. Globalization that does not make the locals better off is a modern cancer. This cancer kills entrepreneurship, innovation, possibilities and talent. Shall we become droids to foreign masters with very different values and interests?

Speak up. Even rage against the machine (one of the best band names ever[23]).

With apologies to Martin Niemöller;

When they came for the activists,
I remained silent;
I was not an activist.
When they locked up the negotiators,
I remained silent;
I was not a negotiator.
When they came for the Chief Executive Officers,
I did not speak out;
I was not a CEO.
When they came for the lawyers,
I remained silent;
I wasn't a lawyer.
When they came for me,
There was no one left to speak out.

Step 4: Seek Diversity:
Bring In Many Perspectives

When you get down to it, you can't know everything about everything. Rather, it is better to surround yourself with experts from a
range of knowledge. They can bring what you don't know in a very
complex industry. That way they can assist you in making the best
decisions. You rely on collaboration for 99 percent
of what you do in business.

Bruce McIntyre, President, Marmac Energy.

When an organization thinks about collaborating, it often assembles the
usual suspects and their managers, who have demonstrated a willingness to get along and arrive at consensus.

But, where are the people who see things differently? If the group norms
dictate that you must be nice and that you must support some project, then
save your energy. The "collaboration" will be shallow and too comfortable.

Given a specific challenge, project or conflict, you must consciously decide
what expertise, personalities, backgrounds and strengths are required. Those
who have different perspectives, expertise, demographics and personalities
are valuable.

"We are looking to create a national corporate funding council. I am at the
national level. We need to bring in people for each province. Am I going to
populate the national council with people like me? No. We are looking for
alchemy through a diversity of backgrounds and perspectives," noted Kyle
Winters, Heart and Stroke Foundation of Canada [24] executive.

In a boardroom, in decision-making, strategic processes or in any similar situation, it is critical to hear contrary opinions. Leaders need to appoint people to actually research and argue the contrary in order to hone the decision so that you've shaved it down to its most powerful impact before the proposal or decision goes out the door. It is not effective simply to be surrounded by people who agree with each other. It is effective to have a diverse circle of opinions and then have the executive—the leader of the team—make an informed decision as to how to proceed.

If you could choose anyone to bring together to collaborate and develop your initiative, who in your past or present would you invite? How might you create the conditions to grow those people in your family, organization, community, nation and world? The bigger game is creating your collaborative culture and making significant positive changes in our world.

Think about the Manhattan Project; perhaps the greatest collaboration involving the greatest minds including Robert Oppenheimer, Neils Bohr, Enrico Fermi, Chien-Shiung Wu and others. It is believed there were 600,000 men and women who worked in the project in the United States, Canada, Britain and elsewhere:[25]

"The Manhattan Project integrated all scientific and engineering fields and was responsible for truly beginning the Atomic Age. Throughout the three-year endeavor, invaluable discoveries were made concerning bomb dynamics and mechanics, materials and plastics, atomic particles, nuclear fission and the beginnings of fusion, uranium, plutonium, and the efficiency of collaboration among multiple scientists and field leaders. Although the goal of the program was not morally humane, the project certainly achieved and surpassed everyone's ambitions."

Think about the things that may have been invented by minds like Albert Einstein or President Franklin Roosevelt, if their intention had not been so focused on the creation and deterrent use of an atomic bomb.

Use tools and knowledge to select and invite in great diversity to convene a full range. Look at personality styles, learning styles, mirror the intended audience/client, bring in those who have little experience, bring in the dreamers, the artists, those that love logic, those who have nothing to gain, the enthusiasts, the marketers.

The key point is to stop bringing in the same old crew that meets routinely on most all the business matters. This must be balanced with: "... the higher the proportion of strangers on the team and the greater the diversity of background and experience, the less likely the team members are to share knowledge or exhibit other collaborative behaviors." *Harvard Business Review* 2007

Everything Looks Like a Nail

If people exercise integrity around the issues that are really a concern to them then you can work on and resolve the issues rather than on defending positions.

Stephen Smith, Inter-Governmental Affairs, Alberta Energy Regulator. [26]

Seeking diversity is, also, an invitation to change the scene. Go outside into nature to shake things up, to shift your brain, to get different perspectives and to generate new creativity. Remind yourself that "if the only tool you have is a hammer then everything looks like a nail." Collaboration, at times and in some circumstances, can be a poor return on investment. A skilled leader will have many tools to apply to given challenges.

If the only place you collaborate is in an office tower sitting around a rectangular table, then topics start to look the same. Get outside. Get active. That alone will bring a diversity of experiences. Collaborate as you sit around a campfire. Collaborate as you walk along the riverside.

According to Paul Born's Tamarack Institute,[27] there are five conditions needed for collective impact. I offer these five conditions here as checkmarks you may reflect on as you read the story:

1. Common agenda

2. Shared measurement

3. Mutually reinforcing activities

4. Continuous communication, and

5. Backbone organizations.

A backbone organization may be an engaged sponsor or executive champion.

Collaboration in the Face of Conflict and Disengagement

The East Kootenay eKnow [28] online digest published a story of collaboration success. It notes:

"Despite many challenges, conflicting interests, a lack of funding and judgments from the outside, a group of 19 people continues to commit themselves to a daunting task. On the evening of September 10, 2013, the Columbia Valley Recreational Access Council (CVRAC) spent several hours as volunteers working to determine fair rights for those seeking access to the areas surrounding Invermere, British Columbia. This group, in its Terms of Reference, hoped to "work toward the development and implementation of a collaborative and cooperative Columbia Valley Recreational Access and Use Plan that is based on preserving and enhancing ecological values of the area and to identify 'best practices' for recreational use in the backcountry and front country." The 19 participants attending the session that evening came with diverse perspectives—as their day jobs included positions in the Columbia Valley Hut Society, Ktunaxa First Nation, Windermere District Farmers Institute, the Regional District of the East Kootenay, Wildsight, Nipika Mountain Resort, District of Invermere, Community Forest Columbia Headwaters, the Village of Radium Hot Springs, the Summit Trail Makers Society, the Columbia Valley Chamber of Commerce and members of the public."

Having a diverse group of committed volunteers prepared to work over extended periods of time (years) to identify and support shared recommendations for recreational use on public lands might seem to many a great gift of service through positive engagement.

The challenge that we are dealing with come from two fronts, political and motorized. They trap us in a Catch 22. Without the government, the motorized sector (quads, ATVs, snowmobiles, trucks…) will not participate. Without the motorized people at the table, the government will not participate. Why wouldn't both participate? Many have argued that the motorized community is better served by dealing directly with the Minister of the Provincial Government (an avid ATVer that represents our local riding). Why negotiate with a group when you have an ally in power?

Secondly, the government (like Goliath of old) misses the connection. In a November 2013 letter to our CVRAC, the Minister of Forests, Lands and Natural Resource Operations for British Columbia tells us: "For the foreseeable future, this ministry will remain focused on key business areas that will enhance the economy of the province. As a result, work around land-use planning is not currently considered a ministry priority and unfortunately we are again unable to dedicate resources to your initiative."

My email back to the Minister stated: "The participants in the Columbia Valley Recreation Access Council are committed to inclusion, engagement and creating recommendations to our Province that are balanced, equitable and serve the economic, environmental and social interests of our valley and our Province. Representatives of the motorized interests are involved and have always been welcome, as all interests are. As facilitator, I ensure that everyone has a voice and no one dominates. When dealing with limited and stretched resources, volunteer citizen and stakeholder groups that work well together do serve as a minimal cost resource multiplier for achieving the Province's goals. The Province's refusal to be even an occasional participant and reference point for the CVRAC is driving the motorized and all groups and individuals to seriously question why they would continue to be actively involved. I believe the 'do nothing' choice at this time will lead to further loses for our Province economically, environmentally and for our communities."

Awareness that the volunteers and this diverse group of people would be undermined by those who feel their interests are better served elsewhere would have been a critical early step for this group to consider (long before they called me in to assist). Like the mediation stages, jumping too soon to solutions is a waste of valuable time and resources. You will come up with answers but you likely didn't ask the right questions. In every collaboration we must be aware of the issues, interests of all affected, resources and where the process may be hijacked.

I am committed to help groups like the CVRAC to come together and serve the public interest, the economy, environment and the community. With a greater focus on threats and opportunities in the planning stage, the CVRAC may have saved themselves from many meetings where their inability to get the motorized community and the government more actively engaged became a great source of frustration. Yes, David can outflank a Goliath. Yes, the motorized community and the provincial employees responsible for environmental protection and approvals likely can be attracted to come together. But for now, the "do no planning means we get to do whatever we want" gives some people the power to decide for the many by default. To be successful, the volunteer group of concerned citizens could have been either more successful or saved themselves a lot of time and resources simply by examining the threats to their success sooner and more deeply.

Volunteers and communities are too often told by politicians how things are and will go. The basis for the democratic process is the opposite. "Power to the People" sang John Lennon. [29] The people actually are the power. Many politicians need to be reminded that, while they do walk a tightrope between representing and leading, ultimately they are always the expression of their community.

While conflict often is seen as a negative, I see conflict as a positive. Conflict reveals those that care about an issue and feel their interests are being negatively affected. When those people reveal themselves, it is far easier to get them engaged in a dialogue. Moving from anger or judgement to a creative dialogue does take skill and patience. But those who stand against are a gift compared to those that do not engage at all.

As time passes and perceptions change, conflict can evolve to engagement.

Collaboration is, also, a powerful motivator for governments to engage and fund. Together with the long-time visionary and dedicated volunteer, Al Skucas, and many others, we are working to complete the TransCanada Trail [30] through the Kootenays connecting Grand Forks to Elkford as part of British Columbia's portion of the national non-motorized trail that connects Canada's Atlantic coast to Canada's Pacific coast to Canada's Arctic coast.

A specific project that Skucas, Neil Shuttleworth and I are leading is in the Kootenays Rockies of BC. Together we are developing another 25-miles/40 km of non-motorized rail to trail from Cranbrook to Wardner. Through presentations and dialogue with local government, business leaders and communities, we have a growing excitement and commitment to get this additional trail completed by 2017. The $1,000,000 it is anticipated to cost will capture a small portion of the Teck Resources Limited's donation through the Trans Canada Trail Foundation, most of it will come locally from organizations and individuals. And that is the way it should be.

We are building a world-class trail system in British Columbia and Canada. Those western Canadians that travel to Europe and the United States to ski, hike and bike on great trails will see active people from those places travelling here to marvel and be active in the majestic natural wonders of the Kootenay Rockies. Governments at all levels are under heavy financial pressures and are retreating from so many of their former responsibilities. Communities, including corporations and not-for-profits must and are filling this need. And for those that focus on "less government is good government" you also must focus on what you can do for your community and the people that are your neighbors. That is unless you are of the "dog-eat-dog" mentality. What is your heart set and that of your community?

What is the culture of your community or organization? Are you more community minded or more independence minded? How would you evaluate threats and opportunities? How might you become more aware earlier on?

For your challenge, project or conflict, what expertise, personalities, backgrounds and strengths will you need? Also, think about your governmental and regulatory leaders, what do they need? Most often they need information, economic and community drivers and reasons to support you. My friend, Rob Gay, is the Chair of the Regional District of the East Kootenay (RDEK). When, during 2014, Al Skucas made application for the RDEK's support including funding, the RDEK slashed the amount by 85 percent. By meeting afterward with elected (and excellent) leaders Rob Gay, Bob Whetham and Heath Slee, we gave them "the information, economic and community drivers and reasons." They asked us to show rural support (not just urban) for the project. We have and they are now providing funding and their endorsement.

When we get frustrated by the failure of people in positions of power, we too often fail to give them the opportunity to let them have our way with us.

We have touched on awareness of threats and opportunities. We have touched on awareness of self. We must also be aware of others, and how we are in relationship with others.

"Googlelization" is a word I created to indicate the at once expensive and at the same time restrictive information we receive from Internet searches. Googleization of our information flow severely limits the nature of the data we are provided and diversity of perspectives we see. We have been warned by Eli Pariser in *Filter Bubbles* that our Internet searches only give us information that is consistent with our previous searches and the content of our online communications. If you don't believe me, seek out two other people in your network who are in different nations, have different networks and different perspectives. Then at a precise pre-arranged moment, each of you search the identical question on the net. A question may be: "Will America ever collaborate with Russia again?" When I search this I get 323 million results. I expect a contact in Russia would get 323 million results as well. And

I expect that others searching will see very different results than mine. Here is your learning opportunity on the effect of the Googelization of the Internet. Seek out two or more very different people from yourself. Different political affiliations, religions, education, nationality, career and other differentiators will help reveal the learning. Ask an agreed upon question and ask it on the same search engine at precisely the same moment. Then have everyone screen capture their first page result. Share these results and discuss what is the same, what is different and why that may be. Then reflect on if and why seeking diversity of perspectives is necessary today for leaders to make great decisions.

In *The Formula: How Algorithms Solve all our Problems...and Create More* by Luke Dormehl[31] we learn that most of us trust the objective and non-judgemental results that a scientific based algorithm provides us as compared to perceptions and judgements of humans. Dormehl, however, warns us that algorithms are constructed by humans and therefore have been shown to be subject to human prejudices, beliefs and judgements. He also warns that algorithms further limit our vision as they severely limit the information we see and the opportunities we are aware of.

Without real diversity of expertise, experience, personality, beliefs, demographics and more, we will have blind spots. We cannot know what we don't know. We are at risk. By actively engaging those that are not like us, do not like our ideas or are paid by us, we may have a more balanced information set from which to lead.

Step 5: Design the Collaboration: Imagine Success and Create the Right Container

Collaborative leadership is the process of opening up space for all stakeholders to be part of an expansive solution.
Denise Chartrand.

Because there is a common misunderstanding as to what collaboration actually is, we need to identify which processes are best.

Notice in the 10 Step process, we have arrived at Step Five and we have yet to get to the place that most leaders start their collaborative efforts. Intention, awareness, embracing conflict, ensuring diversity and designing the collaboration are necessary steps to success. When we rush into it and skip over these conscious preparatory actions, we greatly reduce the probability of breakthrough results. Building an agreement, a business relationship and a culture of collaborative management is significant and deserves far more preparation, planning and engagement than we most often give it. Recall the conditions set by the Tamarack Institute for collective impact. As we think about Alan Gross' words, we start to get granular:

The first step in almost all of these facilitations for me is inclusion—making sure that ALL of the relevant people come to the table. The second step is to guarantee airtime for all to participate and/or to encourage them to participate. Inclusion is related to pre-interviewing, networking, selling the process, etc. Participation is fostered by active facilitation (preventing dominant speakers from taking over;

gently encouraging quieter group members to chime in) and behind the scenes one on one work sometimes during breaks. Breakout groups often help to encourage participation with reports back to the plenary. One of the most important findings from my former field of social psychology is that people who do not participate in group decisions are much less likely to buy into the implementation of such decisions. Sometimes, especially in peace negotiations, these people become known as "spoilers." On several occasions, I have moved/delayed meetings so that everyone could participate ... even those reluctant participants who were busy or said they were busy!

Alan Gross.

Different Spaces:
An Interview with Jeff Cohen

Don't assume all your collaborations must be in a specific space. Interior designers are now creating office rooms specifically for creativity, others for connection, and others for technical focus and more. I find that when clients get stuck, I take them outside. "Walking meetings" are far healthier and creative than those conducted in a windowless office. In 2009 at an Association for Conflict Resolution conference in Chicago we both were presenting at, I interviewed Jeff Cohen on this theme. He gave me further insight into the space design:

My name is Jeff Cohen and I have been a mediator for approximately 20 years. I currently sit on the board of the directors of the Association for Conflict Resolution and am passionate about ethics and raising the bar as to how best to practice this profession and other Alternative Dispute Resolution ("ADR") modalities.

What really comes to mind for me with regard to space is something that I stumbled on a long time ago. The office is not always the best place to be. In fact, I really believe that we should as practitioners take to heart that the office, tie, jacket, and all of those types of things are not where people centers are. If we pay attention to that, sometimes the humility of surroundings—it could be a park, or a mountain, or someone's porch—leave you far better grounded.

Dave: Does that work for litigators and corporate business folks?

"Yes it really does. It's interesting because in my corporate stuff, I don't want to go to their boardroom. I ask them if there's another place they'd like to meet. Now, if they insist on the boardroom, of course I'll do it, but oftentimes you need to get people away from their comfort zones in terms of business if we're going to change the world and the modalities of ADR."

Dave: Wonderful alignment between who you are and what you do.

Collaborative Design Intelligence

Collaborative ventures have the potential for a far greater impact in solving complex problems.

O'Neil Outar.

According to the Economist Intelligence Unit [32], there are five design activities that lead to a successful outcome:

The idea that some forms of collaboration create more value than others is not news. Phrases such as open innovation, mass innovation, co-creation and distributed creation were all invented to distinguish projects that pay big economic and organizational dividends in today's business environment.

Companies seeking to design a powerful collaboration can learn from innovators. Success hinges on whether companies:

1. *Can adopt a commitment to identify and pursue value opportunities.* Successful collaborators recognize there are many types of value opportunities. These include deploying unused or under-utilized assets, finding new and unique applications for assets and employing or combining assets to create discrete new sources of value. They also "know what they do not know," which leads to point #2.

2. *Design effective collaboration.* For example, a company may discover that it needs a process dedicated to identifying and pursuing value opportunities.

3. *Align culture, structure and processes behind value opportunities.* Successful collaborative organizations are unique in the way they deliberately position themselves to pursue value opportunities. They recognize that the existing organizational culture, structure and processes may need to change to accommodate the pursuit of value. They also esteem creativity, expertise and engagement as drivers of success.

4. *Build capacity to fail.* Successful collaborators value "failure" as a critical signpost on the road to success. The corporate capacity to fail encourages experimentation and provides balance in risk verses reward decisions. Failures are seen as a way to focus goals and inform decisions about next steps.

5. *Demonstrate a keenness to "scale up" collaboration.* Those who have reaped the benefits of successful value-seeking collaboration soon become champions of the approach and seek ways to scale it up. They are especially keen to explore how IT can expand the reach of collaboration or introduce its benefits to a wider audience, in some cases via next-generation virtual interactions."

Design and Purpose

Collaboration requires a strong desire and commitment for everyone to win.

Shawne Duperon.

An organization may have any number of reasons to invoke collaboration, which impacts how the process will be designed. Here are some examples:

- Your company is evaluating an acquisition and believes there is unrealized value in the assets/target company.

- You are looking to greater engagement and shared focus with your team.

- Your industry is facing a common threat that requires competitors to work together to address it.

- You are leading a research project and you want to access greater resources.

- You want to change how your organization makes decisions to ensure long-term outcomes are equally recognized with short-term results.

- You wish to improve the delivery and quality of primary health care for patients and providers.

- You are moved by an event/ tragedy/success elsewhere in the world and wish to connect, learn and offer your support.

- You want to shake things up in the way we do things around here by challenging, including and celebrating with more agile networks.

- You are looking for cost reduction opportunities that elude management.

- You believe that others can do part of the job better than you or your organization can.

- You want to find a better way to engage and activate the next generation of leaders.

- You want to kill committees or routine meetings that go on and on and on.

- You want to build trust and cross department/organization/country understanding.

- You are doing research on primitive frogs that still live deep in a cave where you need rappelling experts to get you down and up and a helicopter to get you there.

- You want to build a science project with your seven-year-old daughter and her three classmates.

As you can see, the list is extensive.

And there are many situations where collaboration is the exact wrong thing to do (more on this subject later).

We have summarized the first four steps: Set Intention, Be Aware, Embrace Conflict and Seek Diversity. Now we turn our minds to Design the Collaboration. Each step is important. Creating the appropriate "breathing space" must be conscious and strategic.

Key Design Questions

Consider any of these key "Design the Collaboration" questions to help you establish your own process:

- Why are you really doing this?

- Why would others choose to join us?

- What is the real question that needs to be answered?

- Are the participants' priorities complementary or conflicting?

- What are the alternatives and how do you compare and choose?

- What are the current and necessary preconditions?

- Do you trust the others? Is trust an issue for others? What is needed?

- Is their time line similar?

- What are the underlying interests?

- What is the best alternative to collaborating for everyone individually?

- What will the rules of engagement be?

- How do you encourage disagreement and freedom to speak without invoking negative emotions and responses?

- What about confidentiality?

- What resources do you need to make this work?

- What are the metrics and measurables you seek to create?

- What are the styles of the participants and how do you ensure they are included?

- Who has the authority to agree and how will they be engaged?

- How do you support one another in getting the ultimate result approved within the respective organizations?

- How will this serve you, the others and the organization beyond the specific topic?

- What are the threats? What will pull people away?

- How will people and organizations be accountable?

- What is it we wish to capture as we go through the collaboration?

- What is the physical space that will encourage creativity?

- Will there be times when the group needs to shrink and/or expand?

- How will we communicate with those not directly involved?

- Where and how can we incorporate art, music, poetry, dance, and humor into our circle to engage all parts of our brains, creativity and more?

- What roles do we ask people to play?-

- Who is the facilitator or meeting lead?

- Who will the champions be and when might they change roles within the process?

- What do the executive/stakeholders need to be our champions?

- Shall we invite open source collaboration from experts and others outside our own organization, team, culture or nation?

How External Forces Are Driving Design

In a world where technologies such as smart phones, email and the Cloud make working alone, isolated by both distance and time, the need for collaboration has never been greater.

Pierre Alvarez.

Our world is changing rapidly and the digital age is building collaboration.

One of many exciting innovative online collaborative initiatives was announced September 10, 2013.[33]

"EdX, the online-learning partnership founded by MIT and Harvard University, today announced its partnership with Google to, among other things, jointly develop the edX open-source learning platform, Open edX, expanding the platform's selection of learning tools and worldwide availability. As part of the collaboration with Google, edX plans to build out and operate MOOC.org, a new website that will help educational institutions, businesses and teachers build and host online courses for a global audience. The site—slated to go live next year—will be powered by Open edX and built on Google infrastructure.

"We envision that the site will become an ideal way to develop and refine novel online learning experiences," says Anant Agarwal, President of edX and a professor of electrical engineering and computer science at MIT. "Faculty, for example, new to online learning could get their feet wet, and learners who may not want to take a full course could also just get a taste. Moreover, we will be able to learn how to improve our platform by having more individuals build and use content."

Google will work on the core platform development of Open edX with leading experts from many edX partner institutions, including MIT, Harvard, the University of California at Berkeley, Stanford University, the University of Western Australia, the University of Queensland and Tsinghua University in China.

In addition to technological initiatives, edX and Google will collaborate on research into how students learn and how technology can transform learning and teaching on campus and beyond.

"We have long admired Google's commitment to open access to information, and we believe they will be a perfect partner to work with as we shape the next generation of open education and learning," Agarwal says. "Google shares our mission to improve learning both on campus and online. Working with Google's world-class engineers and technology will enable us to advance online, on-campus and blended learning experiences faster and more effectively than ever before."

EdX, founded in 2012 and headquartered in Cambridge, is a non-profit organization comprised of 28 leading global institutions, called the xConsortium. According to EdX, its aims are to transform online and on-campus learning through novel methodologies, game like experiences and research, among other things".

An estimated 3 billion people have access to the Internet today. With current video conferencing, project management and collaborative software, we have tremendous potential never seen before. With initiatives like edX and Google, we are at the beginning of the age of collaboration. What is possible? Whether we will use those possibilities effectively for the benefit of humankind and our planet is a question worth answering for each person and each organization and each nation. By using all of The 10 Essential Steps to Collaboration, starting with Set Intention, I assert the probability is greater.

Online Collaboration

If one believes the old adage that two heads are better than one, imagine the possibilities of harnessing the creativity and wisdom of thousands enabled by ever faster and more inclusive technology.

Pierre Alvarez.

In the summer of 2013, my son, Dan Savage, and I had an email conversation that went like this: "What if we could go online at any time from our pc, smart phone, IPad or tablet and connect with friends and strangers from around the world to 'listen to one another, to understand, to be curious and courageous and then to create new possibilities.' What if there was a Facebook for 'in the moment' digital video conversations? What if you could log in to a site and connect with a young woman in Connecticut, an elderly Inuit in Resolute Bay, a teacher in Sao Paolo, a sales woman in Seoul, a doctor in Nigeria, a British navy officer at sea? The topic can be anything each one of you had selected before you were brought together?"

This could be a leader wisdom circle of up to 12 people from anywhere around the world. There will be diversity of experience, expertise and interest. Not to debate, but rather, to dialogue.

We might be able to revolutionize the world, to take away the power of divisive media, Mediots, organizations and politicians and to learn that we are not much different from one another. Together, we may understand new perspectives, foreign cultures and values and then devise new strategies to be wiser.

It seems to me that such an online platform is very possible, has the opportunity for people on our planet to hear one another without the filters/barriers that have been present for thousands of years and to create some breakthroughs by collaboration.

Instead of Facebook, let's start a new Internet based on collaboration, problem solving and creativity. Let's revolutionize the conversation. Let's use our collective wisdom and create our shared future. Let's circumvent present networks and mis-leaders.

Step 6: Come Together to Engage with Respect and Trust

Don't give up. The world needs collaboration.
Colin Campbell.

Notice in this ten-step process for collaboration, we do not come together until step 6. Unlike the norm, by taking the time to go through the first five steps, the outcome will be far more likely to succeed. Rushing to "meet" too soon is the equivalent of a "quickie" with your lover; at times just right and most often missing the amazing experience. Take the time it takes to make it the best it can be.

Assuming we all hope to have a healthy economic, environmental and social future life then let's together design how we are and what we do today to create that. We are not separate. We are one. We are one with our past and our future.

This is an invitation to engage with people who care about subjects and questions that matter to you and/or your organization. Your collaborative efforts will be most successful in solving significant challenges or making breakthroughs when you bring in others whose opinion and experiences are very different from yours. The stakes are high. We must invite in aboriginals, the environmentalists, the Americans, the Asians, the youth, the wise women, the artists, the accountants, the "at risk," the enthusiasts, the challengers, the perfectionists and the connectors.

Characteristics of Boundless Collaborations

Dream big and you will create great.

David Savage

- Our intentions must be authentic
- We build relationship and trust first
- We invite and respect diversity of opinion
- We establish key questions that matter
- We listen
- We seek new ideas from the collective wisdom
- We are open to unexpected outcome
- We take as long as it takes, "If you want to go fast, go alone. If you want to go far, go together." *African proverb.*
- We commit to action and hold accountability.

So what are the questions that matter? From our list of significant challenges we face, choose with courage and vision. Remember not to sell or attempt to convince others. Understand what the underlying interests are and be open to what arises.

"Stewardship is about what we can do together to build something great and that we then can be proud of," he says. The best-run organizations "create environments that attract the best and the brightest people. Those people can then use their judgment autonomously to make decisions consistent with the mission and vision of the company."[34]

Rethink the physical space you meet in; does this collaboration invite a circle or a rectangular table, in a boardroom or in nature, surrounded with technology or simplicity. Consciously arrange the meeting place.

Changing the Heart Set

The very best collaborations happen when the team of people have a
high level of respect for and trust in one another.

Linda Matthie.

When you come together, changing the mindset, body set and heart set is important. This cannot be another "bloody meeting." Transition from what you had been doing into a fresh, open and creative energetic space. For most, simply reminding everyone of the intention, purpose and vision may be enough. Some may go outside into nature. Some may use a room that contains artwork, music and large windows and is not the usual meeting space.

Ritual is important but has been much ignored over the past 50 years. Ritual beginnings and endings to collaborative groups serve as important markers to our brain, heart, spirit and body that something different is happening that we need to be open to and aware of.

Realize that collaboration, coaching, dispute resolution and most transformative processes are step changes. They will fail if they are seen as "one time" events. Building, holding and challenging ourselves into a culture of collaboration is very powerful and necessary.

> Few things in life are less efficient than a group of people trying to write a sentence. The advantage of this method is that you end up with something for which you will not be personally blamed.
>
> *Scott Adams, creator of Dilbert.* [35]

Liminal Space

Collaborations bring to each human a fresh perspective with twists on a subject that helps to create new paths within a known framework.
   Tina Spiegel.

Not knowing is an invitation to your team to innovate. Uncertainty is a motivator to change. Curiosity allows us to explore fresh ideas. Openness allows leaders to get out of the way to progress.

In early 2015, I was experiencing a sense of frustration, disappointment and anger over the slow progress of one of my dreams, the Collaborative Global Initiative (CGI). The people we had brought together and their expertise and wisdom excited me for the potential of CGI. I told my co-founders of my thoughts and requests of them. I then stepped aside. For some of my CGI team, they accepted my decision and awaited my return. For others, this was abandonment and rejection. Yet others offered to step up and lead while others simply disconnected. I now understand that I must be very intentional in my communications, as they will be interpreted by others based on their own perspectives and experiences. I also have found that I am loving this freedom to bring my energy back in and focus on my own sustainability and health. This place has allowed me to finally understand that I am not my collaborations. I am not my work. I am not my family. I am me. My collaborations are their own systems of which I am but a part of. I am in the unknown and open to what arises without my direction. Calgary author Deborah Sword advised me that I have created "liminal space."

Liminal space is, according to Father Richard Rohr OFM, who is the Founder of the Centre for Action and Contemplation [36], says, "A unique spiritual position where human beings hate to be but where the Biblical God is always leading them. It is when you have left the tried and true, but have not yet been able to replace it with anything else. It is when you are finally out of the way. It is when you are between your old comfort zone and any possible new answer. If you are not trained in how to hold anxiety, how to live with ambiguity, how to entrust and wait, you will run...anything to flee this terrible cloud of unknowing."

While successful leaders and participants often must be very directive and active, liminal space invites us into a very different relationship to the system or group or issue. Be comfortable with "the terrible cloud of unknowing." Trust and embrace possibility.

Where the Work Is Done

Know, too, that in collaboration, like coaching, dispute resolution and most transformative processes most of the great work is actually done by individuals and smaller groups outside of the room or online session. The "landing" and creating can be even more powerful than inside the physical or digital gathering. Inside the space may simply be where the seeds are planted. The crop may be harvested elsewhere. Very often, I wake up early in the morning with a profound solution to a challenge I had struggled with in my prior business days.

Susan Cain wrote in her bestseller *Quiet: The Power of Introverts in a World that Can't Stop Talking*, "...remember the dangers of the New Groupthink. If it's creativity you're after, ask your employees to solve problems alone before sharing their ideas. If you want the wisdom of the crowd, gather it electronically, or in writing, and make sure people can't see each other's ideas until everyone has had a chance to contribute."[37]

Know, too, the work is never done.

Step 7: Listen Deeply: Realize What Wants to be Heard but Is Not Spoken

I t was once believed that multi-tasking could lead to high performance. Today, we know that "multi-tasking" is a myth as we can only do one thing well in each moment—that we need to focus our attention on the here and now.

This Thing Called Listening

Collaboration requires a strong, clear reason why, an interest, even curiosity on how a better outcome might be possible and listening—with nothing to say.

Bryce Medd, President, Wealthy Tortoise Financial Group, Kelowna, B.C.

There is a reason we have two ears, two eyes, but only one mouth.

Early in my career, when I was participating in boardroom discussions, I would spend most of my time thinking how best to state what I wanted the others to understand. This took me out of the discussion into my own head, and away from the discussion at hand. In doing so, I missed so much opportunity to hear the others and build on the conversations. With my experience and confidence, I soon learned that by listening first and talking later my contributions were far more valued. By having faith that I knew what I wished others to understand after hearing them, I could craft my communications appropriately. "Seek first to understand. Then to be understood."[38].

As a professional coach, I have been trained to;

- Listen at level one: listen to my internal voice.

- Listen at level two: listen with intense focus on the client.

- Listen at level three: sense the entire room and its energy.

Try all three levels of listening. Try it with your wife, husband, friends and colleagues. How well do you really listen? People want to be heard. People want to be witnessed. They deserve your full attention. If you find that you are becoming distracted, are judging, or are already working on solutions, then you are not listening. Let it go and come back in to the conversation. Listen for what is said and what is heard but not said.

If you are really listening, what does your internal voice tell you? Are you able to notice tension or confusion or a deception? What does your intuition inform you of? What doesn't fit with the words being said? What needs clarification?

Consider the Nine Domains, if there is only one person who does not agree, discover what they may teach you. We tend to minimize the dissidents. Instead, explore together what is not understood or accepted.

When the Light Goes On

Often in our formal dispute resolution processes, the process takes charge, the judge takes charge or the panel takes charge. In fact, a significant percentage of disputants leaving court convey their frustration as they feel they were not heard. Mediation serves to rectify this and success comes during two key moments:

1. When the person/organization is finally heard (gets their day in court is the phrase yet it often doesn't happen in court) things change. Once a person is heard and believes the other side understands.

2. When the "light" goes on between the parties. This occurs when both sides realize there is a possibility of agreement that wasn't there before they collaborated.

In collaboration, like negotiation and mediation, the most time must be spent designing, listening, understanding and probing. When you do that, exploring options and possibilities is far more profound and powerful. Time "solving" is the least of all.

Symptom verses Root Cause
You must have the appropriate skill set to accomplish shared goals.
Jeffrey M. Cohen, Esq.

Only by identifying the root cause of a problem might we solve that problem. Quick fixes and failure to find out what the real challenge is lead to the all-too-frequent failure of organizations to eliminate barriers and succeed. Listen deeply, focus on a step-by-step logical assessment and then apply the right fixes.

In 2007 my wife and I purchased a beautiful 1905 heritage home in Cranbrook, British Columbia. We are the fourth owners and love our home. As a renovated heritage home, it has features and new technology such as hot water on demand and radiant heating. During the past eight years, at least twice every year, we have had challenges with the water boiler and system. At least twice a year, a service person has come to our home to investigate and solve the problems. Most always, that has meant buying and installing new parts (controllers, valves and more). In 2008, we had another such event and the service person installed yet another new valve. I left home to travel for business. When my wife returned after work the night the new valve was installed, she called to tell me the house was full of natural gas. She got out of our home and immediately called the service company. They rushed over and fixed the valve. The odor disappeared. Yet the heating system continued to have problems and for years we continued to hire new service people.

It was my intention to find someone who was better at assessing what the problem actually was. But each time the service people made adjustments and sold us more parts. In the summer of 2014, things were getting worse. I had an old natural gas BBQ that had far too much heat. I had asked several technicians and sales people what I could do to reduce the amount of gas coming into the BBQ. No one had ideas that worked. My nephew gave us a new higher end BBQ and, sure enough, that had uncontrollable heat as well. At the same time, our natural gas oven was failing. The temperature would take a long time to get to the levels we needed to prepare food. Again, I called the service company and asked what they could do. By chance, they sent an actual gas technician named Paul. In the first few minutes of Paul being at our home, he said; "Your gas pressure is more than ten times what it should be!"

My first response was, "Why didn't the other service people who have been coming here for the past eight years know that?"

Paul: "I have no idea. We are trained that one of the first things we do is check the pressure."

The pressure at about 70 inches in a residential home is a major problem. Paul tells me we are lucky that we didn't have a bigger problem since it appears the values and controllers simply shut down rather than become wide open. We called the natural gas company and got a technician to come immediately. Upon his arrival, I naturally asked, "Why didn't your company tell us the natural gas regulator was an industrial, not residential, size?" His response was; "We are not responsible for what is inside the home. At times, home owners ask for the high pressure regulators if they have special equipment inside." As you would expect, I was furious! We had been living in a powder keg! With gas leak after gas leak, we had about a dozen service people from three companies come at our request. We had a home full of natural gas once. And, we learn that nobody measured the gas pressure inside our home! Looking back, it is pretty obvious what the problem had been. Looking back, I relied on the "experts" to deal with the problem. Looking back, as a layman, I should have brought out the manuals, spent my own time trying to figure this out. Looking back, for eight years, we had a series of specialists that failed to find the root cause. Instead they dealt with symptoms only.

I share this story because it is a personal and powerful indication of how many intelligent people solve the symptoms and never get to the root cause. If not for a "Paul", how many more invoices and how much longer would we live in a very dangerous home? Who is your Paul in your collaboration? Even the most diverse and talented team can work diligently and fail to identify the root causes. Even I failed to identify the problem. I knew the pressure was too high on the BBQ. I didn't know the regulator was industrial and not residential. I wish I would have asked far more questions and not relied on the experts as much as I did. Once you find your "Paul," listen deeply and serve his interests so you don't lose his expertise and dedication.

The root cause of a problem is what is underneath. In negotiation, collaboration and dispute resolution, we look for the interests underneath the positions. What is the real motivator? What is the real problem?

Step 8: Collaborate with Vision: Tap into the Collective Wisdom

In these troubled, uncertain times, we don't need more command and control; we need better means to engage everyone's intelligence in solving challenges and crises as they arise.
Margaret J. Wheatley [39]

I n collaboration, we are looking to break out of "normal" and break through to fresh and exciting insights and possibilities.

Skating Beyond

Take a sheet of paper or your digital tablet. Draw a skating rink.

When workshop participants are invited to do this, they almost always draw a hockey rink that looks something like this.

Why do we do that? Because most often we skate on hockey rinks. Therefore, a skating rink is a hockey rink. But sometimes we skate on frozen rivers, ponds and lakes. Sometimes we clear a long and winding path around a lake for skaters to have a larger area and a more interesting activity.

Now, draw a place that would be magical for your family to skate in.

Notice that we are open to drawing pathways that go through forests, go up and down slightly, have lots of curves, have creative places for you to sit, have a canopy overhead, may have musicians playing nearby and it looks and feels nothing like a hockey rink. This fresh concept of a wonderful place to skate is nothing like what we first drew. To collaborate with vision, let go of what you think things should be like. Vision invites creativity. Trust and presence encourages our minds to create possibilities beyond what is currently the norm. Vision allows us to break through our limiting perspectives.

See Beyond the Problem

If goals, project timelines and follow-ups are not consistent, collaboration will fail. Everyone within, must know the objectives and what they are solely responsible for in order to achieve the final result. A pat on the back from others or a push in the right direction must be welcomed and encouraged or collaboration will fail.

Aaron Parker.

Too often, organizations get stuck. The reason they get stuck is they do not allow themselves to dream big. They tend to focus on the little and most achievable goals. Or they get so focused on the problem, they never get beyond that problem.

Think about sports and shooting to score a goal. If you focus on the goalie, you will not score. If you focus on the net behind the goalie, that is the target! Seeing the target instead of the problem allows you to achieve.

Another way of thinking of this is high-performance driving. When you drive at high speeds and a collision happens in front of you, you must see past the collision. You see the way through, get your car there and go to the finish line. If you only see the crash or hit the brakes, you will be part of the crash.

Dream Big, then Work Back to Now

When truly opening up to the ideas of others in collaboration, we have the opportunity to go beyond our own rules and beliefs and explore ideas and possibilities that we alone cannot see or choose not to see.

Richard Schultz.

How do we define collaboration? Richard Schultz, leader of *Collaborative Ways*, writes, "At its root it (collaboration) is to 'co-labor' with another, or to work together. This simple idea of working together may be the basis of collaboration but it also conjures up the idea of something more - something of a higher vibration. It is this higher vibration of the word that we want to stretch towards and embrace because in this there are opportunities to expand individual and group consciousness resulting in new behaviors, new solutions and even paradigm shifts."

Be bold in your vision. Look at where you wish to be. Dream about how that feels, what the air is like and what you see there. Dream big. Then work back from there to see the steps to be taken to make it happen. When I am coaching executives, often I must shift them from the day-to-day tension, challenge and frustration. When we explore their values and their vision of themselves and their company in five years' time, they look beyond of the collisions in front of them. They become more strongly motivated. Setting the strategic plan is far easier looking back from success than looking forward past obstacles.

What is your finish line? What do you feel being there? Who is with you? What are you doing? What is your gift? What do you need to do to start building that future?

Stroke and Blocked Brains

In medicine, collaboration is essential for excellence in patient outcomes, medical research and staff working environment. Medicine is a highly person-power oriented discipline that requires one-to-one interactions at multiple levels - patient, colleague, team. There is tremendous intrinsic value in having personnel in medicine who have experience playing in teams or working in teams. Sports is a relevant metaphor because it is important to know as much about what it means to lose as what it means to win, and what it means when losing is not an option.

Dr. Michael Hill, Professor of Neurology, University of Calgary, Alberta.

Collaborate with a vision of world health. I serve the Heart and Stroke Foundation on the Alberta Provincial Advisory Board. Dr. Michael Hill is a past chair of this board. The University of Calgary website describes Dr. Hill's credentials: "Master's degree is in Clinical Epidemiology. He is currently primarily appointed as Professor in the Department of Clinical Neurosciences with cross-appointments to Medicine, Community Health Sciences and Radiology. He currently holds the HBI-Heart and Stroke Foundation of Alberta/NWT/NU Professorship in Stroke Research and is the Director of the Stroke Unit."

I have a profound respect for Dr. Hill's work and his character. He is a leader and a leader in stroke research. Dr. Hill is conducting a study called ESCAPE[40], which stands for "Endovascular Treatment for Small Core and Anterior Circulation Proximal occlusion with Emphasis on minimizing CT to recanalization times. ESCAPE is showing positive results in the international trials. However, the study is at risk of not being properly funded (many millions are needed), given the time (at least five years) or protected from commercialization (drug or medical corporations taking the trial data and making it their very own). The ESCAPE trials, if proven successful, may revolutionize stroke recovery and treatment.

To help us understand, here is what Michael shared with me in early 2014; "Stroke is most often (85 percent of the time) due to a sudden blocked artery in the brain, starving a region of brain of nutrients. If the artery stays blocked, that region of brain dies and there is permanent damage --> a stroke. If the artery can be re-opened in time, under the right conditions, the damage is avoided or minimized. Patients recover. The ESCAPE trial is seeking to demonstrate that opening arteries using angioplasty/stenting (just like we do in the heart arteries) is a better way of doing things than giving clot-busting drugs alone. We enrolled our 100th patient today. We are 25 percent of the way there."

So with Dr. Hill's ESCAPE trials there are huge opportunities, benefits, risks and challenges.

Might collaboration be useful here?

Consider The 10 Essential Steps to Collaboration;

		What
1	Set Intention	To support the ESCAPE trials in support of global stroke treatment without personal reward.
2	Be Aware	There are many heart and stroke research organizations (universities, not-for-profit, corporations and more) who have interests in this type of research and who have not seen my type of public participation, encouragement and fundraising. Crowd funding and funding from non-traditional sources may "contaminate" the research in the eyes of the evaluators.
3	Embrace Conflict	Where may the conflict come from? How may we support ESCAPE rather than get in the way?
4	Seek Diversity	Connect and include a far wider network of supporters, challengers and visionaries than the typical clinical research trials most often experience.
5	Design the Collaboration	
6	Come Together	
7	Listen Deeply	
8	Collaborate with Vision	
9	Now Lead	
10	Make It So	

Notice, I will not complete the steps until I work through the steps. I cannot Design the Collaboration until I get through Seek Diversity and co-create the collaborative.

Complete the table on your own to play with the 10 Steps in this example. Envision you are the convener and you choose to make this collaboration successful. What is needed?

I share this activity with you to underscore my point that our global village has only two degrees of separation. Now that leaders can lead in new ways, we no longer have the option to think or act small. We have opportunities to lead or participate in global collaborations that never existed until this century of humankind. Will my collaborative to support ESCAPE be successful? It will if it reminds us that we are working together on the big issues today.

On February 11, 2015, the Heart and Stroke Foundation of Canada [41] announced;

"New treatment sharply reduces death and disability from major stroke."

Dramatic results from a new clinical trial are set to change the way many strokes are treated in Canada and around the world.

A new treatment was shown to cut in half the death rate from major ischemic strokes in the ESCAPE trial, which was co-funded by the Heart and Stroke Foundation.

Results of the trial, published online Feb. 11 in the *New England Journal of Medicine*, also showed reductions in stroke-related disability.

"This is the most significant and fundamental change in acute ischemic stroke treatment in the last 20 years," says Dr. Michael Hill, senior author of the study and a professor at the University of Calgary's Cumming School of Medicine. "These results will impact stroke care around the world."

The researchers studied 316 people who were diagnosed with a major ischemic stroke, which occurs when a larger artery to the brain becomes blocked by a blood clot.

The researchers found a 50 percent reduction in the overall death rate among the patients who were treated with the ESCAPE Trials ("ET"). The study also showed an increase in positive outcomes for patients to 55 percent from 30 percent.

The team was led by Dr. Hill, the stroke neurologist, and two co-principal investigators—neuroradiologist Dr. Mayank Goyal and stroke neurologist Dr. Andrew Demchuk—all of the University of Calgary. "The ESCAPE trial is very much a collaboration between Stroke Neurology and Neuro-intervention," says Dr. Hill. "It has been a huge team effort."

The Heart and Stroke Foundation provided funding through Dr. Hill's Heart and Stroke Foundation/Hotchkiss Brain Institute Professorship in Stroke Research and Dr. Demchuk's Heart and Stroke Foundation Chair in Stroke Research. Other funders were Alberta Innovates-Health Solutions and Medtronic, along with donors to the Hotchkiss Brain Institute Stroke Team and the Calgary Stroke Program."

You read that this has been a very real collaboration of many different organizations. According to the University of Calgary news release, here are the sites where the research work was conducted collaboratively:

"Foothills Medical Centre, Calgary, Alta.; Royal University Hospital, Saskatoon, Sask.; Colorado Neurological Institute, Denver, Colo.; St. Michael's Hospital, Toronto, Ont.; UPMC Medical Centre, Pittsburgh, Penn.; Queen Elizabeth II HSC, Halifax, NS; Toronto Western Hospital, Toronto, Ont.;University of Alberta Hospital, Edmonton, Alta.; Chattanooga Center for Neurologic Research, Chattanooga, Tenn.; CHUM Hospital Notre Dame, Montreal, Que.; MUSC Medical University of South Carolina, Charleston, SC; Sunnybrook Health Sciences Centre, Toronto, Ont.; Ottawa Hospital, Ottawa, Ont.; London Health Sciences Centre, London, Ont.; McGill University (MNI), Montreal, Que.; Beaumont Hospital, Dublin, Ireland; Abington Memorial Hospital Abington, Penn.;Royal Victoria Hospital, Belfast, N. Ireland; Yonsei University (Severance Hospital), Seoul, South Korea; Samsung Medical Centre, Seoul, South Korea; Keimyung University (Dongsan Medical Centre), Daegu, South Korea; Temple University Hospital, Philadelphia, Penn."

Twenty-two research sites across four countries in three continents; now that's collaboration!

Think about Step 5: Design the Collaboration. How important this was in this multi-site and multi leader ESCAPE project. Think about Step 8: Collaborate with Vision. "The researchers found a 50 percent reduction in the overall death rate among the patients who were treated with ET." Think about the all the costs, personal, family, organizational and financial, of stroke and what Michael and all the participants have realized for us.

Think about your vision and how you will better collaborate.

Consequences of Failing to Tap into Collective Wisdom

Protectionism and ego are the two things that prevent collaboration from even having a start.

Bryce Medd.

How do we hit reset and build relationships, trust, respect, possibilities and a shared vision so that we have, at most, two degrees of separation in our world? I am committed to creating this opportunity.

I advocate for sustainability. Sustainability embraces economy, environment and community, all together at the same time. Sustainability is not any one of the triple bottom lines alone; as long as humanity exists, all three must co-exist. If they don't, in the long term, humans die and environment exists alone.

Pipeline companies, youth, environmental groups, aboriginal communities and taxpayers all have a great role to serve our national interests. Not one of them is "right" alone. Bullying by individual groups cannot be tolerated. The voices of every group must be honored and heard.

I believe that our current way of reviewing applications, consulting the public and determining the public interest creates "Death by Consultation."

During November, 2015, I presented "ReThink Stakeholder Engagement and Regulatory Processes"[42] to leaders of oil, agriculture, ranchers, regulators, environmentalists, legal and more. My message was that, while we have a world respected development application processes and networks, on large proposals to build pipelines, mines, facilities and sea ports, these same systems, far too often, diminish trust, respect, learning, innovation and possibilities that serve the public good. On billion dollar projects, investments of massive amounts of time and money reduce the value of the project. Let's engage and find better ways. We must never accept approvals without proper regulatory, environmental and social review. Yet, where is the balance point between social input, technical input, environmental input, political input, economic input and common sense for the public good? Our processes and systems fail companies, landowners, economics, communities and environment. Collaborative innovation is put aside for adversarial submissions.

For many years now, I have advocated for an enhanced process to examine the facts, the fears, the opportunities, the values, the risks and identify the public interest that serves a clear and sustainable future for our children, grandchildren and great grandchildren.

Here is how you can do this.

- Ask yourself, when you hear the proclamations of special interest groups (on all sides of any controversial project - oil, environment, aboriginal and American included) step back and ask: "Are they providing a balanced or a prejudicial view of the project that serves our/my interests?"

- Reach out to people who have a diversity of knowledge, experience, passion, vision and a love of our economy, community and the planet. Embrace conflict and find the golden nuggets from people who disagree with you.

- Call this diverse group of perspectives into your own learning circle to independently consider a specific project together. I do this with communities and organizations on a wide range of projects, challenges, conflicts and opportunities. It takes time and it takes openness. Decide for yourself. Think for yourself using collaborative learning from people who do not agree with you. Be strong enough to drop your original positions if you find new information that leads you to a new understanding. In my career of bringing people in conflict together, there are two great challenges a) getting them to listen to one another and b) having them carry their new learning and perspectives back to the group or organization they represent. We too often get stuck in being right.

- In this 21st century, we have at most two degrees of separation (not six). Widen your circle to global connections. We have the technology to connect with five billion people today.

- Be an informed courageous leader now. Our world needs you. Our world needs less division, manipulation, positions and self-interest. Our world needs collaborative wisdom that serves us all.

We cannot allow any one group (on any side of an application or idea) to trump all others. As a nation, we must stop the economic, environmental and social media bullies from their behavior that divides us and destroys what we care about most. Come together, decide together then lead this change. We live in a great democratic, resource rich and proud nation.

Rotary Four Way Test

How safe [collaborators] feel on the team affects how they participate..

Sherry Matheson, business coach, Calgary, Alberta

Rotary International (I am a member) has a great Four Way Test to apply to what we choose and how we serve.

Of the things we think, say or do;

1. Is it the TRUTH?

2. Is it FAIR to all concerned?

3. Will it build GOODWILL and BETTER FRIENDSHIPS?

4. Will it be BENEFICIAL to all concerned?

Collaboration well done should meet the Four Way Test .[43] I, also, assert that collaboration is one of the best ways of meeting the Rotary test.

Some years ago when we were living in White Rock, the Cities of Surrey and White Rock, British Columbia approached the three Rotary Clubs on the Semiahmoo Peninsula to discuss how we might assist them in the development of a major athletic facility. The two governments had identified a 100-acre site for development, they had built Softball City in conjunction with Softball BC and Surrey had built the south Surrey Arena on that site. The school district had built the new Semiahmoo High School on the southeast corner and the two levels of government wanted to develop the rest of the site for football, soccer, baseball, rugby and track and field plus build a field house with support facilities such as changing rooms etc. At the time there were minor sports organizations and a Rugby Club which all had vested interests in the development. When brought together to discuss the options the meeting invariably ended up in a brawl with nothing being accomplished. The two cities felt that perhaps Rotarians could moderate the meeting and bring some civility to the discussion to allow for collaboration. Out of sheer stupidity or a genuine belief that Rotarians can bring about change the three clubs agreed to host and chair the meeting. Yours truly was appointed chair.

The meeting was held in the South Surrey Arena with all the parties represented. After a brief introduction and the preamble from the Surrey Parks and Recreation Director regarding the parameters and the amount of capital available etc. the meeting was opened to input from the floor and the fight was on. I finally called a "time out" and warned them that I would adjourn the meeting if after the recess there was no progress. At that point, I left the room in search of a quiet corner to think about what I would do next, and I freely admit that I prayed. I could not think of anything else to do.

Much to my surprise when I returned about 20 minutes later, the user groups were collaborating, they had worked out their differences, each group had identified the areas where they felt that their particular sport could be best accommodated and within a further 30 minutes they had committed a significant amount of their available funds to the project. Within five years the development was complete with all the available space fully developed, it is one of the most successful athletic parks in the lower mainland. Now two of the five Rotary clubs in the area meet weekly in the field house that was constructed with their help in the park.

What changed in that meeting? I have thought about that for years, I believe it was the sudden realization on the part of all the attendees that if they wanted to achieve their goals they had to help the whole group achieve all their goals. None of them could go forward alone, they needed each other and that if they did collaborate they would achieve a greater solution. I'm not sure the Rotarians brought anything new to the table other than a conviction that in order for the greater good to be served the individual wishes of the user groups had to be in harmony with the overall plan and when they all realized that there was unanimity.

—Colin Campbell

When you are ready to decide, act, serve and lead with the results of your collaborative process, check your concept or plan and put it to the test. We can debate as to what truth is. We can decide to act in ways that are not beneficial to all. If so, decide consciously.

Step 9: Lead with Purpose and Accountability

When there is clarity and agreement of fundamental purposes,
then the probability of success improves.
Richard Schultz

Effective collaboration requires the strong leadership brought about by such dimensions as clarity of vision, decision-making capabilities, emotional intelligence, and engendering of trust. A strong leader demands accountability from his whole team, regardless of who is on the team.

Accountability fulfils purpose. What is your and your organization's purpose? What is the essential "why?" you are answering? If you and your organization failed, what would be lost to the outside world? We have talked about how and why collaboration fails or succeeds. But how might you learn from that experience to enhance your probability of success in your present work and in the future?

For a collaboration to achieve and even exceed its goals, everyone, in his own way, must lead. No one can sit idly as a bystander. Everyone, by utilizing his skills and his networks, and so executing on his part of the plan, has a contribution to make. Like a flock of geese on their long flight migrations, one alpha goose doesn't take the point the entire flight. Rather, geese switch out leaders at the front point to allow more to lead into the winds and turbulence while others fall back to the formation to rest while getting prepared to again take the lead. Part of leading with purpose is readying the next generation of leaders on your team or in your organization.

From an online survey I conducted with my corporate clients, I found the following responses dealing with next generation leaders (18—35 years old);

- They collaborate better than we do   64% Yes
- They are more creative than we are   74% Yes
- They have stronger values than we do   88% No
- They are ready to take over   89% No

Through conversations with others over the years, this judgment of the next generation is generally confirmed. Some of my generation judge the next with statements like "lost," "entitled," "not trustworthy" and "self-serving." I think back to my early career and know that my generation was similarly judged. Whatever your perspective, as the current generation of leaders leave, get replaced or die, the next generation is taking over. Why not help them now?

I believe the next generation of leaders is the most talented, connected and distracted generation. I believe we must support their life and career journeys through friendship, mentoring, coaching, training, challenging and accountability.

We must continue to dream, create and lead across multiple silos inside and beyond the walls of organizations. Increasingly, corporations are encouraging their leaders (veteran and new) and people to commit to initiatives that do not have a direct line of sight to specific financial targets for the company. These companies know their future success requires positive engagement and corporate social responsibility with the communities and groups they work in and with. So, if having an engaging shared dream of the future, for leaders both young and old, is not enough, what is necessary to have a high impact?

"The four most significant behaviors consistently demonstrated by high-impact leaders are:

1. defining clear goals or a vision of the future in accordance with the overall organizational aims (the "big picture")

2. creating blueprints for action to achieve those goals

3. using language to build trust, encourage forward thinking and create energy within the team ("powerful conversations")

4. getting the right people involved ("passionate champions").["44]

A major barrier to collaboration is the failure of participants to share and champion the outcome with their own organization, stakeholders, community, political party and/or not-for-profit. Leadership is both the goose at the front of the flight point and it is the goose in the pack. We are all leaders. How often do we truly act as leaders? And how often do we hold back? Is the migration stronger because you are in or if you fall out? Even when a goose falls out of the flight pattern, say due to injury or fatigue, they are not left to die. Others fall out to help that goose come back to the flight group. They support the collaboration need for geese on a long migratory flight. Assuming we choose to lead more effectively and consistently, what is needed? In my Break Through to Yes podcast October 15, 2015-episode Embrace Conflict,[45] I used the peloton metaphor;

"In the Banff Gran Fondo, riding the beautiful Bow Valley Parkway between Banff and Lake Louise, I am not a fast competitive rider. But I am determined and love the endorphins. During the Banff ride, the experienced, fast riders and teams would cut in front of me and it would scare me a bit. I like riding alone. At my own pace. I am slow. There could be a conflict between the fast teams and the slow riders. Think of the peloton where riders tightly group together at high speeds.

According to Wikipedia:[46] "The peloton travels as an integrated unit (similar in some respects to birds flying in formation) with each rider making slight adjustments in response to their adjacent riders (particularly the one in front of each). When developed, riders at the front are exposed to higher loads, and will tend to slip off the front in order to rejoin the pack farther back. With sufficient room to maneuver, this may develop into a fluid situation where the center of the peloton appears to be pushing through its own leading edge."

Speeding groups draft like racecars on the race track and semi-trailers on the highway. In the Banff Fondo, several riders passed me and I decided to keep up. I joined the peloton and it pulled me along. This was so much less work. See how a peloton is a collaboration that makes the long road race much less work for those in it. Think of the Tour de France. Visualise that peloton and collaboration.

So a peloton initially felt like conflict to me then I learned how it made my work easier."

The Competencies of Leadership

Warren Bennis and Joan Goldsmith articulate five competencies of leadership in their book *Learning to Lead: A Workbook on Becoming a Leader.* [47] They are:

"Master The Context: Understand the big picture, be aware of the policy implications of your work, be current on research and reform efforts, and take time to continue to be a learner.

Know Yourself: Be aware of your life patterns, your ability to learn from experience, your heroes who model leadership and your skills in working with conflicts, mistakes and failures.

Create Visions and Communicate Meaningfully: Look to the future, have a passionate commitment to an inspiring vision and be able to communicate this vision so that others are aligned with it and move to implement it.

Empower Others through Empathy, Integrity and Constancy: Build trust through empathy, empower others to be all they can be, take positions of integrity and be consistent in beliefs and actions.

Translate Intention into Action: Bring your vision into reality, demonstrate your commitments, act strategically and realize intention through action."

The Rockyview Project Takeaway— Leadership Is Critical

...organizations hit walls of resistance (partly of their own creation) which prevent collaborations succeeding. The problem is not with the idea of collaboration, but the way many have attempted to apply it. The solution lies in preparing your own organization for the change.

Jonathan Webb[48]

The Rockyview Development is a story of how taking a hard line destroys possibilities, how those positions may be dropped in favor of a new shared vision through collaboration, and what the remaining barriers are that call for better leadership. I'll set the stage for the story with an excerpt from *The Vancouver Sun*, August 27, 2009:[49]

> A move by Cranbrook council to nearly double the size of the city is being challenged by residents who are trying to force a referendum on the plan. Mayor Scott Manjak and all councillors except one support the proposal to add about 3,640 hectares to the east of the city, a move they say will give the city control over future development on the privately held land. "This provides Cranbrook a window of land for next 50 years," Manjak said of the controversial East Hill boundary extension plan. But some dissident residents are trying to stop the project, arguing that the additional land isn't needed for the city. A group called Citizens for a Livable Cranbrook Society held a rally against the East Hill expansion Wednesday outside Cranbrook city hall. Society spokesman Sharon Cross said she was optimistic that her group will sign up the 1,475 names—10 per cent of registered voters—required under provincial legislation to force the city to hold a referendum on proposed changes to its boundaries…She said the proposed expansion is not required to accommodate population growth, saying that the East Kootenays city has grown by only 400 people since 1994.

Both Scott Manjak and Sharon Cross are friends of mine and I respect them both. But the two held strong opposing positions when it came to civic boundary expansion. The mayor clearly wanted to establish greater opportunities for economic growth. The activist clearly wanted to champion a compact livable community.

When the referendum votes were counted, there were 2581 in favor and 2616 against. Of 5197 votes cast, the voting public was virtually tied with only 35 (or 0.67 percent) more on the *No* side. No expansion for Cranbrook.

This issue caused significant animosity amongst Cranbrook residents and those in the region. The *No* side was seen by many on the *Yes* side as anti-business eco-activists. The *Yes* side was seen by many on the *No* side as potentially corrupt developers with no regard to protecting the environment. Neither of these projections was true.

The mayor asked me to work on the issue to find a way to move forward as a community. In late 2010, I agreed to consult the developer, Summit West.

In my report to the Regional District of the East Kootenays and other stakeholders in June 2011, I wrote:

Since January 15th, 2011, Summit West has:
- Invited over two hundred to participate

- Hosted six World Cafés at the St. Eugene facilities for the public

["World Café" is a structured conversational process intended to facilitate open and intimate discussion, and link ideas within a larger group to access the "collective intelligence" or collective wisdom in the room. Participants move between a series of tables where they continue the discussion in response to a set of questions, which are predetermined and focused on the specific goals of each World Café. A café ambience is created in order to facilitate conversation and represent a third place.[50]]

- Hosted two World Cafés with multiple provincial regulatory agencies

- Engaged members of the public plus provincial and regional regulatory agencies in many other conversations

- Placed seven newspaper ads in local media

- Had two articles published in local media

- Spoke to the Chamber of Commerce

- Provided every World Café participant with a Synopsis of the conversations at their World Café

- Provided every World Café participant with a Survey to ensure we get even more advice, and

- Committed to continuing the public engagement program well beyond the submission of the application to the Regional District of the East Kootenay and more.

In today's communities, everyone has something important to add. Effective public engagement requires openness, willingness, persistence, patience and creativity. Effective public engagement, more importantly, makes projects better.

Directly from the six World Cafés to date, we have gathered over five hundred comments, concerns, hopes and recommendations from participants. Summit West has reviewed and provided feedback to every one of the comments.

Summit West is committed to continuing the conversations about this environmentally appropriate and fresh thinking rural community development.

While in January we considered limiting who we invited to the World Cafés due to potential protests, we have found every participant to be genuinely interested in learning about the Rockyview Project and offering their opinions and recommendations. The participants have come from the full range of interests in our region. Everyone was invited to participate as an individual and not as a representative of any organization or group. And all have been invited to express their opinions and recommendations in whatever venue is available to them.

The synopses of each of the six public World Cafés gave a good overview of the discussions that occurred. Overall, early participants came to the Rockyview Project World Cafés with some apprehension and fear from past judgments and perceptions. As the conversations moved forward, Summit West incorporated most all of the public input received. The World Cafés seemed to move into a general sense of "this is very interesting and something attractive for our area." Most participants appear to be supportive of the evolving vision of the Rockyview Project. At the June 7th and 24th World Cafés, the more detailed plans that were created to include the input for prior World Cafés were presented and discussed.

The public pulse around the Rockyview Project seems to indicate "We like this. This is a new approach and planning. This would be an area I would like to live in" (my paraphrase). Another position that was heard early on in the World Café and other discussions are along the "just leave the area undeveloped." This shifted for most to "If Summit West is able to get approval and then builds what has been co-created in these World Cafés, this will be special" (my paraphrase).

Some questions that are important to address and which reflect the main questions of the World Café include:

- What amenities/development opportunities are people excited about for this property?

- What concerns do people have related to development on the Summit West Property?

- What ideas did people have for addressing these concerns?

- What sustainable design features would people like to see embodied in the project?

At a 10,000-foot level the response from the six public World Café participants was--

- This is an innovative and attractive rural community plan

The "hopes" include:

- Will bring new people, new economy and opportunity

- Will bring those who value sustainable living and choose to move/ live here

- Will be a liveable community that brings leading edge technologies and approaches to a "green" rural community

- Allows land use that is not allowed and/or not available in Cranbrook, and

- The plan as it has evolved should have been a part of Cranbrook.

The "concerns" include:

- May take away from Cranbrook, its economy and its sustainability objectives

- Should have mechanisms to ensure it is built and managed consistent with the sustainability themes in its planning and application

- Can't be viewed alone. It will set a new precedent for all future applications.

I believe the Rockyview Project level of public engagement was significant. I believe this report reasonably represent the input and learning from all public engagement on the Rockyview Project that I have been involved in for the period January 15 to June 24th, 2011."

The topics at the five tables of each world café were water, habitat, planning, area benefits/impacts and everything else

Adversaries met at the world cafés and worked together with the developer to completely redesign the rural development. After receiving five hundred comments, the developer evolved its plan to one of the greener community plans in North America.

At the last world café, a man who was a leader of the "No" vote in 2009 and was by then a leader on city council told me "Now, I wish this was in Cranbrook."

As you can see, open and respectful collaboration changed everything, based on the realization that what people participate in creating they will support. And, what a developer thinks the market is seeking is far better tuned to that market when the potential buyers are included in the design of the development.

Summit West could have proceeded to develop rural acreages in the size of five to 25 acres without any approvals. Instead, Summit West sought approval to build 78 homes, a community centre and a central retail and office building that met high environmental design standards for a sustainable community adjacent to the city of Cranbrook, the Community Forest, the Collage of the Rockies, the TransCanada Trail and Highway 3.

In the fall of 2011, Summit West made their zoning application to the Regional District.

So with the shift in sentiment and design, what happened next was unexpected. According to an article written by Sally MacDonald in the *Cranbrook Daily Townsman*,

> A rezoning application by Summit West received first reading at the RDEK board in October 2011. Principal owner Sheldon Isaman presented the proposal to the board.
>
> "I respected the democratic process and results that indicated that the City of Cranbrook did not want to have jurisdiction over these lands and since then we have been working with regional district staff, the public, and professional consultants to further refine the development proposal. The result is what you see before you today," said Isaman in 2011.
>
> However, Interior Health lodged a negative review of the proposal in December 2011.
>
> "This proposal creates a type of urban sprawl which is associated with negative public health outcomes. Research has shown the negative impact of urban sprawl on physical activity opportunities. Physical inactivity often leads to obesity which is directly related to

chronic diseases such as: Type II diabetes, cardiovascular disease, and some cancers," wrote Pam Moore, who works for Interior Health out of Kelowna.

"Interior Health endorses the concept that the built environment influences transportation choices and by association, population health. This proposal specifically … is too remote from any transit route for transit to be a viable option, is too remote from any amenities such as schools or food stores to encourage physical activities such as walking or cycling, [and] its remote location depends on vehicle use and will result in increased vehicle emissions."

The board, which had been newly elected in November 2011, voted 11 to four in favor of referring the application back to staff to continue working with the developer.[51]

An official working for a provincial government agency in a city 530 kms/320 miles away that has an estimated population of 122,000 tells an economically challenged regional district a proposed development that adjoins a city of under 20,000 that, "This proposal specifically … is too remote from any transit route for transit to be a viable option, is too remote from any amenities such as schools or food stores to encourage physical activities such as walking or cycling, [and] its remote location depends on vehicle use and will result in increased vehicle emissions." Note: the lands are immediately adjacent to the city boundary but the current road access is 3 km/2 miles

Does this mean any development outside city boundaries should no longer be approved? That would mean serious limitations for the people of the Regional District, cities, towns and villages within its region. Does this mean that only developments in large urban areas are to be approved? Does this mean that living in cities is healthier than living in green communities just outside those urban centers?

What was shocking to me is the lack of leadership by the Regional District, which did not take a lead in asking these important questions. Instead, it took this last-minute statement from Interior Health as reason enough to send the developer back to the drawing board yet again.

Review my lead statement into this: "The Rockyview Development is a story of how taking a hard line destroys possibilities, how those positions may be dropped in favor of a new shared vision through collaboration, and what the barriers are that remain that call for better leadership." After eight years of trying to develop their land adjacent to the city of Cranbrook, the developers said enough and stopped investing money for planning, engagement, surveys, architects, legal, road building, house building, community building and more. As the area continues to face economic decline, five years later the developers listed the 2,400 acres for sale. These lands will become acreages for the wealthy. These lands will not become a centre of new economic growth.

What might we learn from this about leadership? Where did leadership fail? How might the design better have included Interior Health?

Looking for Heroes in All the Wrong Places

When leaders take back power, when they act as heroes and saviors, they end up exhausted, overwhelmed, and deeply stressed.
Margaret J. Wheatley. [52]

Instead of using shared core values to lead from, too often today, we look for super heroes, rock stars and fictional identities that will separate ourselves from reality and shared possibility.

Those who seek the super woman or super man at the top are always disappointed.

Have you known a superhero at the top of your organization? How did it turn out?

How many leaders do you know who demonstrate an "I know everything" attitude?

Heather Douglas, former President of the Calgary Chamber of Commerce, former Vice President of Athabasca Oil Sands, and current President of Strategic Public Affairs, advised me that to understand clearly and quickly the style and character of a leader, you ask one question: "Tell me the name of the super hero, legendary figure, comic book character or other well-known personality that you strongly connect with." I have asked many people this question in the past decade and find the answers very interesting.

When Heather was an executive with Union Carbide in the 1980s, she asked this question to the incoming President worldwide. His immediate answer was "Hitler." Heather resigned that week. Within a year, Union Carbide laid off thousands around the globe and was responsible for the Bhopal Disaster in India. According to Wikipedia,[53]

The Bhopal disaster, also referred to as the Bhopal gas tragedy, was a gas leak incident in India, considered the world's worst industrial disaster. It occurred on the night of 2–3 December 1984 at the Union Carbide India Limited (UCIL) pesticide plant in Bhopal, Madhya Pradesh. Over 500,000 people were exposed to methyl isocyanate (MIC) gas and other chemicals. The toxic substance made its way in and around the shantytowns located near the plant. Estimates vary on the death toll. The official immediate death toll was 2,259. The government of Madhya Pradesh confirmed a total of 3,787 deaths related to the gas release. Others estimate 8,000 died within two weeks and another 8,000 or more have since died from gas-related diseases. A government affidavit in 2006 stated the leak caused 558,125 injuries including 38,478 temporary partial injuries and approximately 3,900 severely and permanently disabling injuries.

Try Heather's question and see whether and in what ways it serves you. When she asked me this question, I responded that I don't have any single figure that I attach to. I believe in "we."

Granted, at times, a company, a leader, or a President must simply be directive—hard and fast—and hold people accountable. As companies grow, they realize that if they want to attract, retain, and build the best people and the best organization, this is one of the best ways. The best people don't want to work anywhere other than a place where they can learn, be valued and make a real contribution to their organization. Patricia Neal and Craig Neal emphasize this point in their book *The Art of Convening:* [54]

Engagement, and the accountability that grows out of it, occurs when we ask people to be in charge of their own experience and act on the well-being of the whole. Leaders do this by naming a new context and convening people into new conversations through questions that demand personal investment. This is what triggers the choice to be accountable for those things over which we can have power, even though we may have no control. In addition to convening and naming the question, we add listening to the critical role of leadership. Listening may be the single most powerful action the leader can take. Leaders will always be under pressure to speak, but if building social fabric is important, and sustained transformation is the goal, then listening becomes the greater service.

This kind of leadership—convening, naming the question, and listening—is restorative and produces energy rather than consumes it. It is leadership that creates accountability as it confronts people with their freedom. In this way, engagement-centered leaders bring kitchen table and street corner democracy into being.

In every championship team, there is a strong leader with a shared and powerful vision that clearly and repetitively communicates the action plan, the goal and has the skills to lead. In the championship game, the team doesn't huddle together (on the field, at the bench or wherever according to their sport) to start to collaborate on what they should do next. They trust and believe in one another and the coach, captain or quarterback calls the play they have developed and practices together for this exact situation. Like Tai Chi and many martial arts, at this moment in the championship game, how the team performs is deeply embedded in each of their minds, bodies and spirits. This winning play is now a deep habit. The players simply need to be all in. And not thinking they are wishing they had more opportunity to practice or think about their options. The leader leads and is fully expected to lead the team. Everyone is critical to the success of the play.

"Great Leadership Isn't About You," by John Michel in *Harvard Business Review* [55]

The most effective form of leadership is supportive. It is collaborative. It is never assigning a task, role or function to another that we ourselves would not be willing to perform. For all practical purposes, leading well is as simple as remembering to remain others-centered instead of self-centered. To do this, I try to keep these four imperatives in mind:

Listen to other people's ideas, no matter how different they may be from your own: There's ample evidence that the most imaginative and valuable ideas tend not to come from the top of

> an organization, but from within an organization.
> Be open to others opinions; what you hear may
> make the difference between merely being good
> and ultimately becoming great.

Embrace and promote a spirit of selfless service. People, be they employees, customers, constituents or colleagues, are quick to figure out which leaders are truly dedicated to helping them succeed and which are only interested in promoting themselves at others' expense. Be willing to put others' legitimate needs and desires first and trust that they will freely give you the best they have to give.

The Leader as Educator

I subscribe to the thought leadership of Steven Hobbs (DrWELLth). In his book *Help Them Help You Manage—Lead* [56], he describes Nine Educating Approaches (listed below)

Which approaches would serve you best in managing and/or leading? What would you change given different situations?

Instructing: To instruct is to provide a description and explanation of the knowledge and/or skill at a deeper level.

Training: To train is to impart some particular skill with some knowledge for immediate use.

Consulting: To consult is to provide information and/or to exchange ideas.

Coaching: To coach is to drive and/or urge participation through the task.

Shifting: To shift is to support understanding of personal career decisions.

Counselling: To counsel is to talk things over and to listen with caring.

Facilitating: To facilitate is to help a process go well, to draw out from the person/people blue-sky ideas.

Mentoring: To mentor is to provide trusted advice during the adventure.

Minstrelling: To minstrel is to reconcile the other eight educating types through storytelling and fostering the natural rhythms of learning and educating.

Hobbs rightly provides us different ways of educating/leading with adaptability given different situations. How strong are you in each approach and how adaptable are you?

The Dichotomy of Leadership Styles: Collaborative versus Commanding

What follows is an exploration of leadership styles. First, Jackie Rafter, President, Higher Landing Inc., Calgary, Alberta has the floor, followed by Laura Hummelle.

"To Be or Not To Be?" by Jackie Rafter.

Although there are many styles of leadership, one extreme may be referred to as the "collaborative" leader, which is one who makes decision with some degree of collaboration with fellow workers. The other extreme is the "commanding" leader whose decision-making style is usually more independent of the input of others.

The question was, "Which type of leadership style is best? Whether or when does the collaborative leader verses the commanding leader serve an organization best?"

I've pondered this question numerous times upon observing the styles of many business leaders, employers and clients as well as at the onset of my own leadership roles. I always found myself asking, "What do I need to do in order to be as successful as possible here?"

This, of course, is a loaded question. However, I have found that most leaders cannot achieve optimum success without some degree of collaboration, particularly if the corporation's desire is to achieve long-term SUSTAINABILITY. My own experience has shown that it appears difficult—if not impossible—to build a successful and solid foundation without at least some degree of input, contribution and "heart" of key and valued employees.

So, how can you tell what someone's leadership style is? There are hundreds of psychometric, aptitude and personality tests that can usually determine one's leadership style, OR you can observe some common personality traits:

Commanding—often regarded as "Type A," priority is more on making independent decisions verses collaboration with team members.

Collaborative—usually characterized by leading by consensus, engaging the feedback of team members, and making an attempt to understand the personalities, strengths and weaknesses on their team.

So, which leadership style is better? There isn't a "right" or a "wrong" style, for this would require that every person seeking a leadership role conform to a certain stereotype. I have found that there is a place for both leadership styles, in varying degrees, depending upon the goals and objectives of the organization, and even the type of industry.

The commanding leadership style creates efficiencies in circumstances where, for example, an organization needed to be quickly downsized. It may not be necessary (or desirable) to have an overly collaborative-style leader involved with the implementation of the plans—a job has to be done (as unpleasant as it may be) and decisions must be made to ensure the immediate livelihood of the business. I've been in situations where sudden economic changes resulted in considerable lost business, or a major financial restructuring or turnaround was required, and have seen commanding leaders thrive in these environments, often on a "project" type basis. They usually need to act quickly and may not have the luxury of much collaborative time.

Another example of a good fit for a commanding leader would be if the organization's safety or health were at stake. I worked for one company whose co-founder died in a plane accident. After that, a policy was put in place where its senior executives were never allowed to fly together. Although this created occasional inconveniences, the remaining founder insisted this policy be followed religiously at all times, without regard for what others in the company thought. Authoritative styles are ideal for setting certain policies that are assumed to be in the best interest or safety of the corporation—even if others do not concur.

An overly commanding leader charged with building sustainable teams or adding long-term value to an organization may experience difficulty as they face challenges often associated with this style (i.e. high turnover, decisions sometimes made without the "full picture," lost productivity and disengaged employees who are left to speculate on what's going on because they are "left out of the loop" and are worried about their security). When people are merely told what to do or don't feel part of the solution, they usually just show up. It is a lose-lose situation where the corporation never gets the best out of its people. This is not effective leadership and affects everyone, from the mail clerk all the way up to the executive suite. Building long-term, sustainable structures is often where the collaborative leader can shine.

The collaborative verses commanding leader often thrives in situations that are not so "crisis-driven." I've seen numerous examples where an overly commanding leader has made snap decisions with little regard for anyone except the Board or the owner. Although there can be valid reasons for this such as the livelihood of the business, adapting to sudden economic changes or the loss of a major client, the absence of collaboration can also spell long term disaster to the business. In these cases, some degree of collaboration can often get the employees engaged by actually HELPING a corporation through a tough time, rather than running for the exit and more lost productivity at the water cooler. A good collaborative leader would be to take the time to communicate the WHY's of what's happening, and even solicit staff's advice for resolving key business issues such as dealing with suppliers, creditors, marketing a positive spin on the business or landing a new account.

Remember, the negative grapevine is far more potent than the positive one.

In my several years in the executive search business, I've found that collaboration is essential with new hires. It is much better if you can engage several team members in the hiring process for a new employee than make the decision independently. This way you set them up for success and support, their team looks forward to their arrival, and potential threats are minimized. I've seen far too many examples of sales organizations (in particular) where there is more emphasis placed on the top (or bottom) line than the people. This breeds a culture that is highly driven to produce results—which is a good thing—but can also produce a negative domino effect.

For example, you hire someone with a stellar pedigree and track record in another company but fail to engage the input of your own team members. The new "star" doesn't fit your company's culture. You ignore the complaints of team members, good people start resigning, infighting happens, "camps" erupt like mushrooms, productivity diminishes, sales tumble and in the end, you end up terminating your prodigy. Collaborative leaders value and respect the input of their team—and listen to it.

It's easy to make a quick buck off someone that presents him or herself as one that can put some immediate coin in to the corporation's coffers, however if that someone doesn't entirely fit the culture or direction of the company, and ESPECIALLY the personality of his or her supervisor and colleagues, "commanding hires" can result in costly mistakes for the company. Collaboration in the hiring process minimizes the risks of this happening.

It's not easy being a leader of any kind as there is a huge responsibility that goes along with the job and to lives of all who work for them—directly or indirectly. This is a responsibility that should NEVER be taken lightly.

Far too often, we make decisions without collaborating with ourselves by failing to think about the consequences of our own actions, words or thoughts. For every action there's an equal and opposite reaction. I often say, "Our intentions dictate the ultimate success of our actions." I recall saying this to one particular CEO and he seemed very confused, but our own personal motives will always show themselves eventually and will brand our character—for better or worse.

Whatever we're thinking is literally like planning a future event. When we worry, we are planning. When we are appreciating, we are planning. When we think our staff is inept, we are planning. What many leaders fail to recognize is that their thoughts and intentions are usually far more transparent than they realize—especially with social media and the office grapevine. It is for this reason that WHATEVER your leadership style is, being transparent, honest, up front and engaging the input of your team wins you far more brownie points and company loyalty than wearing your cards too close to your chest.

In my experience, people—the right people—are the core of building a successful, sustainable business. And it is very difficult to achieve this without engaging the input of others in important decisions such as key hires, strategies and the implementation of important initiatives. A collaborative style is usually more effective at unleashing the potential of people, stimulating creativity (a critical success factor) and inspiring them to achieve more than they—or you—ever thought possible. It is a gift to be a leader. Therefore be kind, be collaborative and engage the hearts of all those you are fortunate to lead.

They say two minds are better than one. For that matter, so are 20 or 200.

"An Organization Needs a Vision for Collaboration," by Laura Hummelle.

In the past, leadership was relatively simple. Leaders at the top of hierarchies oftentimes become leaders because they were able to make good decisions for their organization. But then came the second half of the twentieth century, which saw the rejection of the formal hierarchical structure. But because organizations often failed to replace this structure, such organizations often suffered from what came to be known as the "tyranny of structurelessness." Often, in these situations, fundamental things like who made decisions about which issues and who was accountable for what things weren't clarified. This led to an increased number of raw, informal hierarchies and conflicts that resulted in the failing of many of these experiments and eventually gave "flat structures" a bad name.

Command-and-control leaders took charge and were typically seen as controlling, mechanistic, autonomous, self-preserving, and resistant to change. They bury contradictions, value position and structures, hold formal positions, set rules, make decisions and wish to know all within the organization.

Over the years, though, this leadership style has declined in effectiveness. As the world changes and evolves, things tend to get more complex. Increased complexity makes it harder for one or a few people at the top of an organization to be able to sense, know, understand or process the information in ways required by the environment. The higher volumes and increased complexity of information necessitates more processing, through more perceptual filters and diverse perspectives of more people. So more input from more people is required to enable hierarchical organizations to respond adequately to a more complex environment.

This shift tends to be accompanied by a corresponding shift in people's values where people want or demand more of a say in decisions, and things like inclusion, participation, diversity, equality, collaboration, and cooperation are given more value.

Companies have moved to integrate cooperation, delegation of authority, shared decision-making, individual and team autonomy, consultation and participation in creating visions, etc. However, in a hierarchy, the underlying structure on which all of this is founded means that, at any time, people higher up the hierarchy normally have the power to trump the delegated authority, shared decision-making, and autonomy of those lower down. So this type of collaboration is always partial, conditional and able to be withdrawn. It is often a desire to transform this power differential into something more equitable that fuels the shift to more flat structures.

Before defining collaborative leadership, an organization first needs to define collaboration and the activities that collaboration entails. Do some research—review information about collaboration and why it is important. Look at what other organizations are doing. What business trends might make collaboration even more important? Understand business drivers and evaluate and mitigate risks. Identify what would be the benefit of greater collaboration for the organization? Create an iterative (not a grand plan) collaboration vision statement reflecting how improved collaboration would advance your organization's vision and strategic priorities as they relate to the main trends in the industry and how they affect your business.

The attributes of a collaborative leader most often include modeling a learning culture, teaching others, coaching, facilitating, asking questions and espousing a willingness to be vulnerable (in not having all the answers and in the context of learning).

The New Role of Leaders

Following on the themes presented by Jackie and Laura, here is an excerpt from Kenneth Cloke's fine book *The Dance of Opposites; Explorations in Mediation, Dialogue and Conflict Resolution Systems Design.* [57]

Fundamentally, the role of leaders in an organizational democracy is to expand the number of degrees of organizational freedom and orchestrate these elements to create learning relationships that link people across artificial boundaries. Organizational separations and divisions that are not integrated produce role confusions, feelings of irresponsibility, misunderstandings, stereotypes, conflicts, and internal dissension, which can be used to justify and rationalize bureaucratic divisions and hierarchical control. Every organizational division is simply a different way of understanding, processing and solving common problems. The task of democratic leaders is to reveal the whole to each of its parts and to integrate the concerns of all into a single synergistic, strategically integrated whole.

Collaboration, democracy, and self-management are prerequisites for evolution to higher levels of organizational development based on synergy, community, and strategic integration. Through these processes, it becomes possible to build creative, motivated, high performance, self-managing teams that harmonize and orchestrate a wide range of organizational skills, strategies, systems, processes, and relationships to produce synergistic results.

Creating a fully democratic, collaborative, self-managing organization requires more than fragmented, step-by-step, tactical reforms. It requires integrated, holistic, strategic transformations that increase diversity, complexity, synergy, and interconnectedness and challenge everyone to operate at their highest levels of effectiveness. In the process, employees need to become owners of the organizations they are changing and of the process by which they are changed.

An Awakening

While the word is not yet spoken, you are the master of it; when once it is spoken, it is the master of you.

Arab Proverb

A critical aspect of collaborative leadership is mindfulness, as discussed by The Honorable Judge Hugh F. Landerkin, QC., retired Judge, Parksville, British Columbia, in this excerpt from *Non-Adversarial Judging: You and the Theory of U.*[58]

Dialog comes from the words "dia" meaning through, and "logos," meaning the word. Physicist David Bohm tells us that three basic conditions are required for effective dialog:

1. All participants "suspend" their assumptions, literally to hold them "as if suspended before us"

2. All participants must regard one another as colleagues; and

3. There must be a "Facilitator" present who "holds the context" of the dialog.

I see the role of the judge in the Settlement Conference[59] as the person who "holds the context" during the whole of the conference. When the judge does this, the flow of the conference goes in a natural way, with the judge guiding everyone, often in a nuanced way, forward. Hence, my descriptor of the Settlement Conference is that of a dynamic process.

As in mediation, there is a natural flow in the process that *The Theory of U* presents. You observe constantly to gain a sense of the disputants, their positions, interests, and wants. Employing dialogue as your method, and by giving everyone a chance to speak, to "talk story," you start to see what is going on within the dispute.

Paradoxically, if you understand basic communication skills, you know that the most important thing is to learn to hear what is not being said, as non-verbal communication in the Western world approximates about 75 percent of our normal communication. Reading the real story is the art of the intervener. The judge's greatest tool for this may be the use of silence. There is an ancient Arab proverb that guides the judge: "While the word is not yet spoken, you are the master of it; when once it is spoken, it is the master of you."

For a judge schooled in advocacy, who uses the spoken word to persuade, coax and convince, remaining silent in an interactive Settlement Conference is surely difficult. As Oscar Wilde, remarked: "To do nothing at all is the most difficult thing to do in the world." Perhaps the judge can gain wisdom from Sir Winston Churchill: "Courage is what it takes to stand up and speak: courage is also what it takes to sit down and listen."

As an intervener, you have come into the process at the invitation of the disputants, and as a guest you have "Suspended" your own personal beliefs. You have learned to "Let Go." Your ego is left outside the room, and now your only interest is in working with the parties to redirect their views, invariably, which start as positions, to their real interests. You begin to get them on the problem- solving road and then to do one of the hardest things for people generally, and disputants in particular, you lead them to let go of their past. If you haven't yet learned to let go yourself, they will never be able "to mirror" your own conduct and let go themselves. A facilitative judge will practice this: an evaluative judge cannot.

Eckhart Tolle, in his now famous book, *A New Earth Awakening to Your Life's Purpose* [60] , tells a story about letting go. Two Buddhist monks, Tanzan (the elder) and Ekido (the younger) were walking home to their monastery on a wet and muddy trail, as it had been raining heavily in their district. Near a village, they came upon an old woman who was looking at the swiftly flowing creek she needed to cross, as did the monks. Tanzan asked if he could assist her across by carrying her on his back and she immediately consented, whereupon Tanzan slowly, feeling the stones beneath him, made it to the other side with Ekido following. Tanzan let her down gently, she thanked him for his kindness, and the two monks carried on in silence. Several hours later as they approached their monastery, Ekido could no longer restrain himself and asked Tanzan why he had carried this woman across the creek, adding, Zen monks are not supposed to do things like that. Tanzan's reply is worth noting and remembering: "I put the old woman down hours ago, are you still carrying her?" The Roman philosopher Seneca teaches us that each new day gives us an opportunity to render a kindness. This is all that Tanzan did, yet Ekido demonstrated an inability to understand this, and to let go.

As a judge, I had to constantly discipline myself in this stage of the "Letting Go" process, for I recognized that as a human being, I had biases, views, and opinions which could affect good human as well as legal judgment. I had to let go of these traits and train myself to be what mediator Kenneth Cloke calls "omnipartial"—partial to all.

The hardest goal in a mediation process, and, I believe, in any negotiation, is to find the mutually agreed on problem definition, the MPD. It is only when we come to learn more about the underlying sources of an apparent dispute, the "back story," that we see the real story about the conflict. We can then understand the actual problem, move forward, and now work on solutions.

I would like to think that I was moving towards what Dr. Thomas Homer-Dixon calls "A prospective mind," a mind not fixed on the status quo, one that is instead comfortable with constant change, radical surprise, even breakdown . . . and must constantly anticipate a wide variety of futures. With a prospective mind, we're better able to turn surprise and breakdown, when they happen, to our advantage.[61]

Mindfulness

We create more reliable and resilient organizations by focusing on sense-making and collective mindfulness when "the world" values individual accountability, predictability and hard evidence for decision-making.

Laura Hummelle

As I learned from Sherri Savage, teacher, Kelowna, British Columbia, leaders in education are bringing mindfulness to early education in future leaders lives though programs such as MindUP™.[6263] Utilizing MindUP™ in the classroom allows teachers to help kids maintain focused attention, form more accurate perceptions of students, think more clearly especially under pressure, improve communication with students, parents and staff, improve the overall classroom climate by infusing it with optimism and hope, help to create a stronger, more vibrant school culture, be happier, more joyful and grateful—a disposition that ultimately spills out of the classroom and into private life and experience greater job satisfaction."

To be inclusive, curious and complete, leaders must increasingly embrace mindfulness to enable themselves to be open to other perspectives and possibilities, and to keep the reactive-focused reptilian brain in balance.

This is a concept understood by the McKinsey Company. At the top of the corporate food chain, organizations and executives seek out McKinsey. The company is self-described as "the trusted adviser and counselor to many of the world's most influential businesses and institutions...the creation of knowledge supports McKinsey's core mission: helping our clients achieve distinctive, lasting, and substantial performance improvements." Perhaps the most effective program McKinsey offers is *Centered Leadership*.

In March 2014, McKinsey's Joanna Barsh and Johanne Lavoie published *Centered Leadership: Leading with Purpose, Clarity, and Impact*.[64] Here are aspects of mindfulness and leadership as described by the authors:

> Through interviews, teaching, and consulting, they uncovered what distinguishes the most effective leaders. Simply put, the answer lies in how leaders lead themselves and take accountability for their personal and professional growth in today's challenging environment. At the heart of Centered Leadership lies the practice of self-awareness and choice. The ability of leaders to be mindful and at choice in the moment helps them tap into purpose and vision

(Meaning), shift habitual patterns into a learning stance (Framing), create collective relationships (Connecting), step up with intention (Engaging), and sustain transformational growth (Energizing).

Mindfulness, intention, openness and/or presence are the spaces for creation. I have been told that our monkey minds remind us who we are between 8,000 and 14,000 times every day. The monkey mind is that incessant chatter that holds us to our busyness and judgment of self and others. What would happen to you if your monkey mind did not tell you who you are so often? What might be possible in the space of not knowing and un-certainty? That less full mind might allow new thoughts, feelings and perspectives.

"The only thing that interferes with my learning is my education." Albert Einstein [65]

Think about the phrase "Let go and let come." This may have come from the phrase "Let go and let God." God, spirit, intuition or your own inner knowledge, it doesn't really matter. What matters is that we access as much of our intelligence as we may. To stick within the logical, conscious mind fails to provide us the other wisdoms. Barsh and Lavoie also write:

> It's scary to be great. It's scary even to dare to be great. It's damn scary. We all long to be seen and heard by someone; to make a difference. But in that moment when we are seen and heard, we are vulnerable. We are naked. Don't waste that moment. Greatness lies within waiting for you to bring it forth. When you do, weird as this sounds, and it was certainly weird when I experienced it personally, you may feel tremendous love and kindness for all living things. You may feel the boundaries dissolve between you and everyone else, everything else in the universe. I groped for the words to describe that experience of joy, hope and lightness of being. Ralph Waldo Emerson described it well over a hundred years ago:
>
> "In the woods, we return to reason and faith. There I feel that nothing can befall me in life; no disgrace, no calamity, leaving me my eyes which nature cannot repair. Standing on the bare ground my head bathed by the blithe air and uplifted into infinite space, all mean egotism vanishes. I become a transparent eyeball. I am nothing. I see all. The currents of the universal being circulate through me. I am part or particle of God."

Four Buddhist Virtues

The most important choice we can make is between fear and love. As far as I'm concerned that's the only two choices we have. If we choose love, we're always going to put the team first and we're always going to have better results ourselves because of it.

Chuck Rose

Emerson's words, as quoted in Centered Leadership, evoke the Buddha, and to close this chapter on leading with purpose and accountability, we reinforce the concept of centeredness as it is so important to understanding collaborative leadership.

The brahmavihāras (sublime attitudes, "abodes of brahma") are a series of four Buddhist virtues and the meditation practices made to cultivate them. They are also known as the four immeasurables. According to the Metta Sutta, Shākyamuni Buddha held that cultivation of the four immeasurables has the power to cause the practitioner to be reborn into a Brahma realm. The meditator is instructed to radiate out to all beings in all directions the mental states of:

1. Loving-kindness or benevolence

2. Compassion

3. Empathetic joy

4. Equanimity

The four immeasurables are also found in Patañjali's Yoga Sutras, a text composed long after the beginning of Buddhism and substantially influenced by Buddhism. These virtues are also highly regarded by Buddhists as powerful antidotes to negative mental states (nonvirtues) such as avarice, anger and pride.[66]

Step 10: Make It So: Positively Change the Energy and the Future Together

It's the 'opening' energy that I now seek more often in relationships
and collaborative situations. After all, the way I see it, collaboration
isn't an external entity we build but is more an internal opening toward how we approach one another, or an internal closing,
depending how the relationships are viewed, valued and handled.
Tammy Dewar, Founder of Raising the Village, British Columbia

There is a fine balance required to be a successful collaborative leader. At
once you are called to be open and inclusive while at the same time taking
charge. People need to believe in their leader and in their team.

Is the best leader the rock star or the leader who places others in the recognition spotlight? I say both. Each is optimal in certain circumstances.

To "Make It So," you will need to design and follow through on:

A) Accountabilities

B) Reporting

C) Continuous improvement, post-mortem, what worked, what didn't,
how are we together now, what is needed for future collaborations

D) Building the collaborative muscle of your organization

E) Learning from successes and failures

F) Using accepted evaluation tools, and

G) Integration—changing the existing ways we do things to capitalize on the collaborative process, outcomes and the organization's rules of engagement. Build your culture of collaboration according to circumstance and need.

Mother Earth Is Stripped

We bought this property because we had a passion for the land and what we could do with it. We have lived simply and even sold our family home to make the purchase possible.

Monelle Fraser, Manager, Human Resources, Calgary, Alberta

Imagine a beautiful diverse forested mountain landscape on the eastern slopes of the Rocky Mountains. Consider your dream is to build a small eco-lodge in this quiet green space. In the future, you see families coming from the city to reconnect with nature and themselves. Consider the wonder of a child seeing, for the very first time the Milky Way, even the northern lights, in the deep darkness away from any city lights.

Your dream is shattered with the declaration "You better sell since we are getting ready to blow up these rock faces and strip mine for coal. Why would you want to live next door to a dirty strip mine?"

I was called in October 2014 by a professional negotiator to see whether I could assist the landowners who were so threatened by an international mining conglomerate.

I met with the landowners whose mountain retreat lands are immediately adjacent to the proposed strip mine. After I completed my due diligence, we agreed to work together to level the playing field in the negotiations between the Australian Asian Mining Company and the landowners. I tend to fight for the underdog when it appears the bad guys are set to win. I am a career natural resource explorer and developer. And I am an environmentalist. I believe our connection to Mother Earth is sacred and will work with industry, with community, with environmentalists, with politicians and more. I refuse to be put in any one of those boxes.

Leaders, especially collaborative leaders, cannot sit by as one group is pushed hard by another with much greater resources. We must "Make It So." Our values, respect, accountability must be held in our negotiations. They cannot be set aside because you may be working for the people your client wants to win over.

In these times, development, including industrial development, degrades some part of nature and wilderness to serve the demands of a world population for food, energy, shelter and more. Such degradation flies in the face of ecological diversity that is a critical part of a healthy life support system for humans as well as the elk, grizzly, badgers, squirrels, ants and eagles.

At what point do we daily ask the bigger question: "What is more important? The wilderness or business? What is more important, the watershed and natural spaces or metallurgical coal? Metallurgical coal is shipped to Asia to build cars and trucks. Do we need more cars and trucks? What is the value of the wilderness? In planning, economics, evaluations and negotiations, we are taught to make the highest value and best use for land as our focus. How do we measure that? How do you compare a net present value of hundreds of millions of dollars for a coal strip mine to the value of nature left alone? Strip mines in the mountains are not reclaimed and restored decades later as mountains. It is most often a flat plain of toxic sand. There is no guarantee that says, "Don't worry, once we are finished with our business, we will clean up the land and put it back into the original condition we found it."

While the executive of the Australian coal mining company was personable, the interests of the company and those of the landowners were very different. After a number of meetings, conversations and emails over several months, I confirmed again with the executive that he had "refused our repeated requests for a written guarantee of year-round road access to the landowners' land, and to compensate them for their time and expenses to respond to your application. Until this is rectified, we will no longer attempt to collaborate and negotiate with you. Six months of positive communication has gained them nothing. Should you be prepared to guarantee access in writing and reimburse them for costs, we shall then re-engage. We understand that the future access will be different based on your mining plans. Nonetheless, we believe a written commitment is critical to making any progress. My attempts to seek a collaborative negotiation had not yet succeeded."

As word started to circulate that the coal company may close the only access road to the area, more and more landowners started to collaborate. We worked together to ensure every landowner had a voice and took appropriate steps with any regulatory body to register their concerns.

In April 2015 in the town of Blairmore, Alberta, the coal company hosted an Open House to update stakeholders on their progress and plans. We now had eight families registering concern and more. We also had two companies register concern with the authorities over access and other issues. One was an oil company hoping to abandon and reclaim well sites, and the other was a renewable energy company hoping to construct a hydro and wind farm. It was standing room only at the Open House in the Elks Hall. Some folks were there to find out what was going on. Others were angry and wanted to vent. Some wanted to see the town grow again and provide decent jobs. Some were aghast that the company thought strip mining a wilderness area for coal to send to India, Japan, Korea and China was even being considered. I approached the company executives to talk a few times during the event, as did the eight landowner families.

I went back over to the coal executive and suggested that as a new starting place we could together work out a written letter of how we engage, communicate and negotiate going forward. I suggested that the Community Relations Adviser would be helpful in guiding us both on Alberta Energy Regulator expectations. The coal executive didn't respond except to say, "We are always ready to meet to talk." This line found no favor amongst the landowners as they feel the limited talk had done nothing to date and had given them little confidence that their interests would be taken seriously by the coal miners. If they could at least guarantee the landowners access to their lands, they would then have one barrier removed in negotiations. From my 40 years of experience in oil and gas, I have never seen something like a threatened road closure and isolation used by a proponent as a tactic to get his own way.

I share this event to show how a collaborative negotiation too often moves into a regulatory or litigation conflict. By ignoring the fears and amount of time and money spent by landowners who have propriety rights next door to the proposed strip mine, they went from a minor issue and cost to build trust and confidence in the relationship. They may now find they have a multi-year battle carried on by lawyers and regulators costing hundreds of thousands of dollars that will put their entire project at risk (along with their credibility and the confidence of their investors). It is not my business to decide whether coal strip mines are built on the slopes of the Rocky Mountains. It is my business to ensure everyone has the opportunity to be heard, the relationship is created and those directly involved on all sides find ways to work it out together. But that night in Blairmore, those that were "pro" and those who were "con" not only did not have the opportunity to talk with one another to find out that there is no pro or con, there is whatever we choose to negotiate and create together.

Do I want small towns to prosper, be a great home to future generations and be welcoming to others? Yes, in the strongest terms. I live in one. Do I see ways of accomplishing this? Yes, in the strongest terms. I have volunteered a significant portion of my time to regional sustainable economic development. Do I know there are far better ways to collaborate and resolve conflicts? Undeniably. Can we do that by deciding differently than in the past? Yes.

The conversations in that Open House were more along the lines of "are we prepared to sacrifice some people's interests and our natural environment to create employment here for the next 25 years?"

I do not believe this is the mindset that creates opportunities; this antiquated mindset fosters conflict by people taking sides.

Too often, leaders see themselves and the possibilities for their organizations and communities only in the rear view mirror or from a scarcity mindset. Collaboration, given the right conditions, will create unexpected and significantly positive consequences. I believe corporations that embrace sustainability and serve the public's needs, prosper.

What is the highest and best use of lands on the slopes of the Rocky Mountains? It depends on one's perspective. That of the wildlife, the shareholders of the company, the under-employed in the nearby towns, the "public" at large. We must relook at this question and determine how society decides. An answer that was acceptable decades ago, we will likely find, is not acceptable today. Who is collaborating on that question and its impacts?

When a company is seeking to obtain the legal rights to strip mine a large area of wilderness, who has the authority to speak in that conversation and regulatory tribunal? Do we need to blockade roads and tarnish industry to get invited to those negotiations? How can we collaborate with the coal mining company, the local and state/provincial authorities and interested parties? That is a question that should be put through The 10 Essential Steps to Collaboration. What is our intention based on what values? Around the world, we do have excellent regulatory project review and approval processes. The threat and real uncertainty of cumulative impact is coming now. How may we collaborate to determine what new thresholds, metrics, engagement, natural economics and more are appropriate today? These questions are at once challenging and necessary. I believe that we must redesign our processes and systems. For both the proponent and the opponent, the systems are too long, too expensive and fail to bring people together in positive innovative relationships.

"The promise of applying complexity science to business has undoubtedly been held up by managers' reluctance to see the world as it is. Where complexity exists, managers have always created models and mechanisms that wish it away. It is much easier to make decisions with fewer variables and a straightforward understanding of cause-and-effect. Here, the shareholder value philosophy, which determines so much of how our corporations operate these days, is the perfect example. Placing a rigid priority on maximizing shareholder returns makes things clear for decision-makers and relieves them of considering difficult trade-offs. Of course we know that constantly dialing down expenses and investments to boost short-term margins inevitably damages the long-term health of the company. It takes a complexity approach to keep competing values and priorities and the effects of decisions on all of them in view—and not just for management, but equally for investors, analysts, and regulators."[67]

Effective Collaborative Meetings

I think that we're on the cusp of having to break into a deeper understanding of collaboration and what it really takes to do that because we have to both be assertive to our positions…We also have to be cooperative. We have to listen to those other voices as well.

Kathy Porter

Meetings are the spaces where collaboration, negotiation, leadership and accountability are central. Too often, though, none of that occurs. To some executives, collaboration is manipulation in disguise. For example, one of my clients asked me to attend her company's weekly management meeting so that I might gain some insights. After the meeting, I presented this President with a sketch on a pad of paper. I explained that the big rectangle was the boardroom table and the small circles around it represented the people in the meeting. She was at the head. Throughout the hour-long meeting, I simply drew a communication line. That line started with the person speaking and connected to the person being spoken to. If three people were being spoken to, three connecting lines were drawn. Further, I added an arrow to show the direction of the talk (i.e., from whom and to whom). I pointed out to the President that in the sixty minutes, almost all of the lines had arrows from her to two other executives. Less than 15 percent of the lines had arrows to her. And very few lines came from any of the other dozen people around the table. I asked her what that illustrated to her and what she may wish to change. She asked me to give her the paper and she would talk with me later. She was genuinely surprised and wanted to think about what I had drawn. How many meetings do you "attend" rather than collaborate in? (Step 3: Embrace diversity, bring in many perspectives.)

Do toxic leadership, backstabbing, competition gone wrong and, for some, being a deer in the headlights (or a hiker in a tunnel with train coming fast in your direction) characterize "normal" meetings?

In *American Icon: Alan Mulally and the Fight to Save the Ford Motor Company*, Bryce Hoffman tells of such destructive dynamics as the way Ford executives met for many years. That is, until Alan Mulally got there. Mulally demanded honest accountability and the focus on "we," not I. It took the executive several weekly meetings before one executive decided he was likely to be fired anyway so he might as well tell the truth. Mulally cheered rather than chided. Slowly others found the courage to become a team and tell the truth.[68]

Here is my quick guide to using The 10 Essential Steps to Collaboration to chair a meeting. This works for small and medium-size meetings. If the meeting is large (i.e., more than 15) collaboration must be designed differently including breakout groups on specific parts of the challenge or objective. In large groups the willingness and ability to have effective collaborative communication is more difficult. It is better in large meetings to declare the topic and allow smaller groups to work the topic.

Step #	Step Name	Thoughts
1	Set Intention	Be honest. What is your purpose? What is the reason to collaborate? Why this and no other strategies?
2	Be Aware	Engage others. Don't speak at them. Ask far more questions than you make declarations. Even if you are certain of the solution or outcome, invite others and support their growth and leadership.
3	Embrace Conflict	To ensure there is constructive criticism, appoint some of the participants to find the holes, the gaps, the pitfalls, the unintended consequences and the errors in whatever the meeting is developing.
4	Seek Diversity	Who is affected by this? Who has different expertise and may see
5	Design the Collaboration	What is our past experience on this matter with these participants? What are our options other than or outside this meeting? What are our rules of engagement? What are the communication, leadership, conflict styles of the participants and how do we blend or connect them to for the greatest chance of success? Who are the ones that don't need to be directly involved? How do you show them respect while not including them? Is there a timing and layering approach as we move forward so the participants will shift roles and come in and out? Can we compress the time? Can we meet outdoors? Should we meet with clients, customers, or other departments that will be affected later? What are the learning and mentoring outcomes that we want to be a part of this? Should we have a "shadow" chair to observe the energy, dynamics, and non-verbal actions in the room and address them?

6	Come Together	What are our rules of engagement, accountabilities, and objectives? Does everyone not only understand them but also respect them? Who is taking up too much of the space? And who is taking too little? How do we test our decisions? What is the most effective way to address the weaknesses that we observe. Do we have a ritual or practice to start the meeting so everyone "switches" on to this objective and leaves the rest out of mind for now? And how do we conclude our meetings to capture decisions, action plans, accountabilities and targets? Do we rate our meetings and our own participation at the end so we can be seen as truthful, willing to improve and even better connect as a team?
7	Listen Deeply	Am I listening to not only what is being said but also what is underneath and to understand previously unknown connections and reliances? When I think I understand them, how do I test them with the group? How do we capture and build on insights together?
8	Collaborate with Vision	Put away the glasses that you wear most often. Look at the topic, challenge, opportunity, people . . . from the future. Take a look at it as if looking at a valley from the top of a mountain. Feel the vision. Before you commit to a specific action, plan or decision, always ask three more questions (and invite others to ask them) to test the merits of your plan.
9	Now Lead	Communicate clearly your understanding, the reasons why this is important, the reasons for your decision and the next steps you plan to take. Engage others in the execution of the plan. Engage others in the experience of the coming success. Now is the time to take charge and lead.

10	Make It So	In this meeting and long afterwards, seek continuous improvement, learning, collaboration, accountability, communication and leadership. Show by doing. Show that this matters by removing those that are not performing and adding those that will.

Each of the 10 Steps is important. And within each of the 10 Steps, look for opportunities to practice each of the 10 Steps. While completing Step 10: Make It So (and focusing on accountability), listen deeply for what is being said by your team or team member for what is underneath. As you make it so on this particular initiative, evolve the collaborative culture of your organization for readiness and improvement on future collaborative projects. What worked well? What needs improvement? Are there members that need to be removed or developed?

As a collaborative leader, recognize and celebrate the team's success. And when the collaboration fails, be personally accountable.

Walking in Circles and Spirals (What We Can Learn from High-Performing Teams)

The goal of collaborative leadership is to create positive new futures by working together.

Denise Chartrand

While the professional sports leagues find marketing a select few of their "superstar athletes" to be a great strategy to engage fans and sell tickets, those athletes will be the first to tell you they depend heavily on their team for success. Think of your favorite team sport. Think about the great come-from-behind victories or an exceptional display of athleticism. Whether you play or watch basketball, baseball, football, hockey or soccer, you understand that winning is a team effort. Very occasionally one athlete may control the play and take the ball (or puck) from one end of the court or field to the other and score. Most often, however, that athlete will be foiled. Those athletes become the targets of the other team and are the lonely ones in their own dressing rooms.

My son, Dan Savage, played all sorts of aggressive team sports in his youth. One of his hockey teammates was an excellent skater and liked to keep the puck for himself. When summer came and the sport turned to lacrosse, that same teammate tried being the "show"—only once. On his first shift, he was hit so hard by a player on the other team, he flew backward in the air. He learned his lesson and from that moment on he decided that passing was the best way to win. He and the team went to the provincial championships that year.

Play your position, play as a team, play as you have practiced and know we win as a team.

In your organization, play your position, play as a team, practice, play as you practice and win as a team. But note how two things that are necessities of winning teams in sports are slow to become part of the winning formula for corporations. Practice: how, and how often, do you and your team practice negotiations, meetings, conflict resolution, operations and simulations? In the past twenty years, our organizations have practiced safety drills, fire drills, CPR (Cardiac Pulmonary Resuscitation) and working through simulations. While we practice safety, we rarely practice any other equally important procedures, processes and skills.

The second thing that sports teaches us that is of value to organizations, yet slow to be adopted, is coaching. Coaching and practicing go hand in hand. Coaching helps us see other perspectives, creates new visual goals and allows us to try out different ways of doing the same thing to see how the results may differ given different people and situations. At every level from the front line to the corner office, coaching and practicing greatly enhance our probability of making the best choices and developing and managing relationships.

Or you can choose to be the solitary superstar at the top that repels those you need to succeed. Think in the context of the lacrosse player being rocked off his feet by the other team by trying win by himself. In the twenty-first century, we love the "rock stars" of music, politics, sports and entertainment. Now we have another visual of a "rock star"—the guy flying backwards in the air after getting rocked.

The Why and the How

True collaboration requires risk taking. When people don't feel safe and comfortable, they don't really open up or show up with their entire integrated self. When you come from a place of integrity, can be clear about what you actually mean and have the confidence to know what you know, then you are available to listen deeply to other people.

Esther Bleuel, Tough Talk Coach, Thousand Oaks, California

As I worked with my publisher and editors to complete this book, many of our early discussions included this pitch:

> Most industry or department heads know and understand the importance of collaboration, but many lack direction on how to accomplish it. They now have a definitive resource to build a collaborative culture that empowers breakthrough thinking for all associated with their organization. David Savage has been a businessman leading teams for forty years. During that time, he has seen repeated failures that arise through conflict, misunderstanding, misalignment of the organization and its leadership, lost productivity, wasted time and wasted resources— all of which damage the success of the organization.

Yes, I have seen many failures. I have been the leader in many failed attempts to collaboration. This is one of the key reasons I wrote this book. This is a key reason for much of my work; helping leaders work together with great outcomes. I refuse to walk on the straight and narrow. And, at times, I walk in circles.

By walking in circles, I am speaking about walking with people around the world in mutually supportive relationships. And I am talking about not giving up when things go badly or attain only small success. The evolution of collaborative leadership and collaborative cultures takes time, resources, patience and determination. For all the initiatives that have failed, they also have increased our understanding of collaboration and the breakthroughs it may create. Practice, practice, practice—and, while doing so, search for the best processes and people for future collaborations. Building our skills and our successes is not a straight line. We go round and round while each time getting closer to our true target.

Successful collaboration initiatives do not cease or see their impact falling off over time. In other words, if you go through all 10 steps, launch, drink the champagne but then abandon the initiative, that result cannot be called a success unless your intention was to have a limited-term outcome. Look at the process, the 10 steps, the relationships and the results over time. Did your collaboration generate positive results over time and in the outcomes, as planned? We must not continue to work together, launch, abandon then launch something new. We must consider the long-term suitability of our results and design for that.

The original design spoken of in Step 5 may be seen as the "getting to" design, but the sustaining thereafter is very important. While I suggest you incorporate the suitability and ongoing service of a collaboration as your start with Step 1, "Set Intention," in addition, at prescribed times post launch, go back through the 10 Steps to check in, reset, redesign, and lead going forward. This is more than a post- mortem project review (i.e., how did we do?). This is an ongoing collaboration.

Collaboration as a means to launch a start-up organization that involves participants with already busy work schedules in their current organizations is one of the very most difficult to design, lead and sustain. Considering the start-up initiatives discussed above, here is one measure of their success.

I, also, actively collaborate for change through the Heart and Stroke Foundation, Rotary International, the Canadian Association of Petroleum Landmen, the Petroleum Joint Venture Association, the Canadian Association of Professional Speakers and in the past many industry and professional associations. With these well-established groups, my measure is what my contribution is to the objectives of the organization and how it also serves my own interests, my community and our world. With established groups, my role is far different; more project and special initiatives collaborations that easily fit within the ten steps. My role is not a founder/senior leader role in those organizations.

I am more prone to invest my time, knowledge and resources in start-ups when I see clear gaps between what is needed and what is available. Think about what type of organization and in what circumstances your intentions, interests, generosity and dreams are best served.

> In 1905, Paul Harris, seeing a need, and desiring a stronger business community founded a new organization for networking and community service.

> Our 1.2 million-member organization started with the vision of one man—Paul P. Harris. The Chicago attorney formed one of the world's first service organizations, the Rotary Club of Chicago, on 23 February 1905 as a place where professionals with diverse backgrounds could exchange

ideas and form meaningful, lifelong friendships.
Rotary's name came from the group's early
practice of rotating meetings among the offices
of each member.

*"Whatever Rotary may mean to us, to the world it
will be known by the results it achieves."*
Paul Harris[69]

What are the results you wish to achieve and who are the people you need to make it so?

The Hallmarks of Successful Collaboration

It was always easy to say, "We don't want to include the voices of our enemies. We just want to include the voices that agree with us." Unfortunately, I would say a rule of conflict is if you try to not include someone then they're going to find a way to be included later.

Duncan Autrey, Collaborative Global Initiative Co-Founder,
Buenos Aires, Argentina

Most readers of this book are crafting their skills to collaborate better on initiatives (which often are within and outside your organization) with known processes, resources and roles. This may give you a sense that it may be easier than collaborating on a start-up. And that assumption may hold you back from changing all the rules and relationships. There are costs and benefits of each manner of collaborative initiative. Ensure you are conscious of the factors at play and design with the end in mind.

To build your skill and network, start with specific challenges and opportunities within your own organization(s). Start small and build the confidence of your team that collaboration works better than the other approaches to getting things done and achieving goals.

What is one challenge or opportunity that I commit to break through and capture by using a confluence of people, organizations, resources and structures? Confluence?—"A coming or flowing together, meeting, or gathering at one point." Given this intention and objective, forgetting for a while our own structure, resources and limitations, what is the optimal confluence of people, resources, processes and global networks that will achieve success?

When I speak of walking in circles, often a successful collaboration takes a long time to occur. Unlike simply calling a meeting on a specific task, successful collaboration requires the participants to have the awareness and skills to collaborate. Sometimes, we must accept baby steps even when we know much greater steps are possible. With this book, I want to create a better bridge between the vision and the action. Effective collaboration is evolutionary. Every time we work together, we are developing our own story, network, behaviors and possibilities for future collaborations.

Depending on the perspective we take, the movement is different. When we talk about walking in circles, with a view looking down, the movement is around and around seemingly without progression. Yet, if we look at the same movement from the side, it may be seen as a spiral rising upwards as we move.

If we keep the effort of collaboration small or controlled, we will keep having the same small and controlled result. Continuously, like an upward spiral, review what is working well, what needs improvement, who is working well together, who doesn't fit the team. Are we getting enough courageous participants who challenge the ideas, is the collaboration designed as well as it could be and do our reward systems support the people? By looking at the circle continuously it becomes a spiral to better collaborations over time. Collaboration is not an event; it is a culture.

Old Ways and Little Steps

To become an asymmetrical organization—to embark upon a more collaborative mindset systemically across the entire workforce—is to invoke participation and input from everyone (as necessary) as opposed to always (and only) commanding and controlling. It is introducing an imbalance to a tiresome relic of the 20th century. The leadership hierarchy is still required, but hierarchy for the sake of hierarchy and antiquated "command and control" habits are most certainly not ideas that will champion a collaborative workforce.

Dan Pontefract[70]

Think about old technology. How does it get significantly improved? There are reports across the globe of how when the windows and doors of an organization get thrown wide open, the world answers the challenge and finds solutions that were not happening in the closed shop environment.

Think about Tesla breaking rules and giving away its technology. Open sourcing builds better vehicles, increases loyalty and leads to higher profits. Playing within your organizational silo and collaborating small is understandable, yet, the leaders who are developing their collaborative leadership, networks and aspirations have a great advantage. And those that play only within their own organization are missing opportunities they fail to recognize.

Think about doing far more with less. Think not about brick buildings and procedure manuals. Think instead about relationships, innovation and creating possibilities never realized before. Think about developing agile, flexible and high-performance teams that access collective intelligence.

Start small, learn together, build trust, empower the group, celebrate success and learn from failure. Dream big and, to recycle another phrase, "Think Global and Act Local." And consider these words from Everett Cox, Veterans Advocate, New York: "The first collaboration for every human being is in the womb. The first collaborator for every human being is a woman. When that first collaborator is dishonored in any way the entire social fabric that began at the womb is threatened, weakened, and endangered."

Tina Spiegel advises that "collaboration is likely to fail if any of the above key elements are not sufficiently nourished during the process and as a result do not grow to support the collaboration." She goes on to say:

> Another cause for failure is when the people collaborating do not include all the stakeholders to the project about which the collaboration is being conducted. We have probably all experienced this event either at the time of collaboration or implementation of its outcome.
>
> In public domain collaborations, the difference between information and knowledge often creates a large divide between the participants. Today, information is readily available on the net in many forms. As a result, we feel and believe we are well informed. We may be, but to turn that information into knowledge requires not only wisdom but experience relating to the area of expertise which the information addresses. It takes time and patience to deliver some knowledge to those of us who have only information to give to the collaborative process. Frequently the time is not available and those of us who are only informed do not recognize the need for the

transition to knowledge and wisdom. In other words, the time and funding is not available to make the playing field level. This situation is frequently faced in the collaborative process of public participation in town planning, which of course deals with issues in the public domain.

According to *The Economist*, for collaborative projects to succeed, each team member must:

- Be competent and committed
- Have a clear line of sight to strategy
- Be keen to share exclusive/sensitive information
- Value expertise highly and preferably bring unique expertise to the table
- Be convinced the project will benefit their company (and themselves)
- Applaud and value creativity
- Have a high level of trust in other team members.[71]

My experience with my own collaborative initiatives shows that no matter if all of the above ingredients are in the mix, the collaboration will not thrive without strong leadership, commitment to change, systems and accountability. With great intentions, shared values, complementary skills and a clear vision, teams and projects can still fail. Collaborations fail because we/I have confusion on where strong leadership and successful collaboration meet. If we are asking others to participate as equals and we/I don't also exert certain command-and-control behaviors, the team muddles along. We can't accept tourists on our collaborative train. Collaboration tourists are those who ride along but do not actively and continuously energize the work.

Remember why collaborations fail?

- Lack of Trust
- Belief that you must know all to be credible
- Manipulation as collaboration
- Failure to challenge

- Lack of diversity of expertise
- Poor follow through and accountability
- Abandonment after project success or failure
- Poor learning loops
- Hiring, performance management and compensation objectives and systems not aligned
- A naïve belief that collaboration is always good. A failure to assess the other options before choosing collaboration.

So, what is the answer? What is the antidote to failure? It lies in the Leadership Mastery Circle. Here's a short story about the Canadian Nuclear Association to illustrate the point:

Horrified

"They were horrified!" Dr. Jason told me.

"We obviously touched a nerve. That is a start" I replied.

"That is an interesting perspective," stated Dr. Jason.

"Tell me why they are horrified?" I asked.

"They feel that you are asking far too much. They say they are too busy to do this. They will not make time. They just wanted a keynote speaker."

"And what do you think, Jason?" I inquired.

"I believe this work is important and already your coaching has changed how I perceive our needs as an organization. I am now journaling and reassessing my role."

"This is a good start, then."

The Canadian Nuclear Association had approached me to speak at their annual conference in Ontario. The topic was effective stakeholder engagement. When asked, I said, "No, and here is my counter-proposal. We arrange a conference call with a few key members of your organization's board of directors to talk about your interests and aspirations." During the subsequent conference call, I asked: "What is your pain? And what is the medication that you feel best heals your pain?"

"Our pain is that no one likes us or trusts us. Our nuclear power plants are aging. And we will never build another nuclear facility in North America again.

"Our medication is to hire speakers to go into stakeholder communities and tell them our story."

I responded, "I agree with your pain description. But I disagree with your prescribed medication. Before you can 'tell them,' however, the nuclear industry must earn the right to that conversation. Earning that right starts with listening to your stakeholders' interests, fears, aspirations and concerns."

In a later conference call, I shared my beliefs that one-time presentations and speeches at best make people look at a fresh perspective or idea. Within a day or a month, that idea or perspective is lost through our busyness with our own work. By working together in round tables/circles over time, building awareness of ourselves, our organizations, our communities and our world, we can then begin to assess what is most important to us and what is most important to those same groupings we are a living part of. With clear intention, we may then practice a new way of leading, influencing and being in our world.

I proposed the Canadian nuclear industry start a Leadership Mastery Circle. This would allow up to twenty key people to meet once a month for at least six months to build their fresh awareness of themselves, their industry and their possibilities in the world. Each month, I would coach each participant individually. And the circle would be confidential exploration of interests, challenges, accountability, dreams and future possibilities.

But that was what "horrified" them. Too busy. Not a priority. Don't really know what you are talking about. Dr. Jason said, "I have realized we don't even know who we are let alone how to connect with our stakeholders. We have never looked at our work from this holistic perspective."

I believe in transforming organizations through embracing all perspectives, all wisdoms and all realms by building awareness of self and others, realizing the importance of values and curiosity in leadership and evolving over time. Real positive and significant change does not come any other way.

I ask too much of my clients because I want so much for my clients. And I do not want to waste time with coaching and facilitating leaders who are not courageous. This writing is also for me to explore; am I delusional or exceptional? I think both. I believe I hold a space for transformation. And I know my bank account suffers for it. Many peers tell me—you ask too much. Others tell me, take them in baby steps if that is what they need. I write to share and to take a new perspective.

Oil Corp. and Negotiation Mastery Circles

Walking into the downtown boardroom of Oil Corp. (a fictional name for a large Canadian-based multinational oil and gas company), I expected to meet with one Vice President. I quickly realized this was not the case when faced with six senior executives sitting around the large oak table. "Dave, we are interested in your Negotiation Mastery Circle (NM Circles). Tell us about them." After summarizing my monthly NM Circles, I asked them the reason for their interest. "We want you to bring a Negotiation Mastery Circle into our organization."

I said, "No." Their surprise was evident. They rarely heard "No." Their eyes told me I hit a nerve. Oil Corp.'s top negotiator/trouble shooter asked me why. I replied, "Because your organization doesn't negotiate; Oil Corp. dictates. Further, you turn the negotiators in your organization into messengers."

I further offered, "Should you ever decide to challenge your executive, management and negotiators to truly be open to changing negotiation within and outside the corporation, then I am ready to work with you." After a few moments the man with the most authority spoke, "We want to get more from our negotiators. We want to change the culture within this organization."

Now, I have been in the Canadian oil and gas business for most of my career since 1975. With my background knowledge, I knew their culture and their great success. I told them, "You are a very successful explorer and producer in Canada and in the world. And you have accomplished that with a very strong executive team who manages with a tight hand. What makes you want to change?"

They gave me four meaningful responses:

1. We are now far too large to direct everything from the top down;

2. We agree that our negotiators are mostly messengers and we would like that to change;

3. Most of us will retire in the next two to 10 years, and we need to ensure those that remain behind are equipped to carry on; and

4. We spend far too much time fighting fires that is, resolving conflicts that come up when things go wrong. Things are going wrong more frequently.

Considering this, I countered with an offer to design a Negotiation Mastery Circle specifically to meet their needs. I told them, "This will be a significant challenge for the negotiators and especially for you six and the balance of the executives."

I also insisted that success of the program depended on their commitment to the following:

- The change process;

- Encouragement of your negotiators to challenge them;

- Full participation in the circles; and

- One-on-one coaching with me.

I then warned them: "You must, also, realize that this will take time. Secondly, when your negotiators start challenging you and things feel out of kilter, that means it's working. To get better negotiators you must lose some control. "

The lead man asked, "Dave, will you do five Negotiation Mastery Circles within our organization starting in the next two months?"

And my answer changed to "yes" as I was suddenly excited by the possibilities.

This personal experience with a company whose top executives claimed they wanted change demonstrates just how difficult cultural transition is. The source of the difficulty comes from the essence of the task: Getting people to change their behavior. Life is a negotiation. Corporations are the people within them. And seldom do organizations attend to the negotiation of how those people will be with one another. Conflict is avoided, people fit in and groupthink is embraced. In Step 10, "Make It So," you as leader and change agent must be patient. Look for incremental improvements and look for ways to align desired behaviors with communication, accountability, compensation and culture.

Critical to strong relationships is Attachment Theory. [72] No matter what, I've got your back. The quality of a person, a relationship and leadership is reflected by what happens when shit happens.

It takes time and it takes the right people. People need to be held accountable for the wrong behaviors, and if those behaviors continue, they need to be taken off the work (or out of the organization). Organizational development is not an excuse for poor performance. And, at times, the poor performance comes from the top. In one NM Circle, an executive challenged me on why he should waste his time on this. I asked him if he thought this was a waste of his time. He said yes. I said, "Leave now, please." This shocked the people in the group and the other executives. I have no patience for those that grandstand and try to take control. If he truly had better things to do, then he better get to them.

I designed my NM Circles based on my belief that behavior change comes from growing awareness, exploration, commitment, practice and steps toward success over time. Every NM Circle participant is asked to commit over a minimum six-month period to meeting as a circle of up to twenty individuals once a month for four hours, individual private coaching, journaling, reading about best practices, checking in with authenticity, declaring their intentions, supporting the circle (and all others in their circle) and practice building awareness of themselves and others. These are the tasks that lead to their growing negotiation and leadership success. We learn to watch each other's back, to challenge one another and to trust one another.

I bring negotiation mastery from an inside out approach. I find books, strategies and tools rarely productive. All too often, in negotiations, we poorly prepare, avoid conflict and make small deals. I believe conflict is positive in many ways. It indicates an organization employs and supports people who speak up for what is most important—their values and those of their communities and stakeholders. A high-functioning team or organization finds their wisdom through adversarial perspectives. A high-performing organization also embraces all personality strengths and styles. The different perspectives allow the organization to experience the planned outcomes internally before the proposal or plan goes out the door. Leaders who embrace diverse perspectives and challengers from within will find their culture dynamic, agile and successful. This is the culture change I hoped for Oil Corp.

Before starting the five NM Circles, I surveyed the 75 negotiators and managers from locations in Calgary and Fort McMurray, Canada. I conducted and videotaped one-on-one interviews with key persons. I used this information to customize my materials for Oil Corp.

Organizations often hire me to lead Negotiation Mastery Circles with their own negotiators, leaders and future leaders inside their offices. They believe that with this, they will be able to make better deals with other companies or groups. This is true. And once we get going (usually by the second month) they find that most of the negotiation challenge topics they wish to work on revolve around negotiations within their organization. The negotiations within our organizations are the most needed and least attended to. And the most difficult negotiations are those with ourselves. Here is a graphic I created to present the realms of negotiation.

The management announcement to the seventy-five included, "In support of our mission statement 'to develop people to work together, Oil Corp. will be running a negotiation training program. The intent of this program is to strengthen the negotiation skills of our staff through greater awareness, empowerment and accountability for the outcomes of negotiations whether they are with internal or external parties. Our objective is to increase our value by creating clearer authority, responsibility and accountability for you in negotiations. We believe we can make significant improvement as an organization in this area and therefore are committing both the leadership as the selected participants to making this an important initiative and focus over the next several months."

The sentiment in their statement to "develop people to work together" is clear. What that looks like in practice is often very challenging for many leaders. My perspective and that of the Nine Domains work I do is that a highly functioning team is one where constructive criticism, push backs, challenges and diverse opinions are highly valued, encouraged and used to build better outcomes. A high-functioning team is rarely comprised of "Yes, Sir" conflict avoiders. A key role for me as lead in the Negotiation Mastery Circles is to "incite insurgency" as a member of a previous Savage NMC declared. I work to reenergize participants to challenge themselves, their teams and their organizations in ways not often seen. Progress is made as team members move from comfort to deep review to challenge to reflection to new insights and then to better and more sustainable deals and strategies.

While leading the five NMCs and coaching the seventy-five participants, the majority of participants embraced the opportunity to be seen, to improve themselves and to strengthen their role at Oil Corp. After many sessions, I heard comments such as "After working here for several years, this is the conversation I have been waiting for."

On the other hand, resistance and discomfort with my NM Circles approach also arose, especially in the executive sponsors. Feedback from some included: "Why are we spending so much time listening to people?" "This is different from what I was expecting."

One participant offered his view that the Negotiation Mastery Circle was really a "circle of scepticism." He did not have faith that Oil Corp. was really prepared to change its culture. I encouraged him that change takes courage and time and that he among others at all levels must lead in this change; this is his work and his life. I told him, as I learned from Margaret Wheatley, the word "management" must be replaced with "leadership." When asked for her definition of leadership, Margaret's reply was, "Anyone in an organization that sees a challenge and leads others to a solution." This perspective on leadership serves to open up organizations at all levels.

A number of Oil Corp.'s key staff talked to me individually about some of the missed opportunities, unethical dealings and possible significant cost savings. I coached them on how to deal with these issues within Oil Corp. to make positive changes.

After three full months of Negotiation Mastery Circles, accountability calls, individual coaching, homework, journaling and reading, I heard very mixed reviews of the five Negotiation Mastery Circles from the Oil Corp. executives. Two said, "It was a joke" or "Like therapy." I spoke of the very challenges and resistance we anticipated back in December, that transformation and culture change takes time and that we must be open to more than the logical left-brain, short-term approaches tried unsuccessfully by others. I reminded them that when it gets uncomfortable for them, it is working in building the engagement and skill of their negotiators.

I challenged the four executives in the room to do as they committed to six months prior:

- Be open to different ways

- Notice what is shifting

- See what is and is not serving them now

- Encourage others to challenge the mantra, "This is the way things are done around here."

This is a real-life negotiation with yourself, your team, your organization and your boss, I underlined.

There were no sessions, coaching calls or sessions scheduled for the summer months. The NM Circles were to resume in September. A few weeks before we were set to restart, I received an email from my main contact at Oil Corp. stating: "To maximize the benefit to Oil Corp. staff participating in the program, we feel that more focus on developing negotiation skills, specifically in the areas of strategy, tactics and tools, is required…"

In my Negotiation Mastery Circle Level 1 program, at the completion we include a celebration of learning and success where with art, humor, song, story-telling, music, poetry, spreadsheets or whatever each group or participant chooses they have some fun, be creative and further lock in their learning. In the Oil Corp. email, there was also a statement that we would not be doing the celebration of learning. Rather, "We would like to focus on Oil Corp. case studies of successful negotiations and poorly executed ones with the lessons learned from each. We will come up with the case studies (real examples) and engage those that were involved with those negotiations to present these cases to the whole group."

Oil Corp. was uncomfortable with the holistic approach I bring to negotiation and leadership training. It did not understand how having people personally check in at each circle and challenge "the way we do things around here" as having any clear positive relationship to Oil Corp.'s deal-making success. My incitement was to challenge the mantra of "the way we do things around here."

To make room for others to take responsibility, control and authority, leaders must give up some of their responsibility, control and authority. To do this requires trust. Trust must be earned over time. When a leader doesn't trust his staff or feels insecure with giving up some of their power, collaborative leadership fails.

By email and conversation, Oil Corp. told me to focus on tactics and case studies. I responded by noting: "Oil Corp. is already very good at strategies and tactics. Our objective is to make negotiation mastery real at every level. Every participant has a different learning style, people learn through their own lens, and different people have different learning styles. Changing the negotiations and the corporate culture are complementary goals. This will not occur with even more of the same. We need to find the sweet spot that will engage all individuals and teams to this change." In a conference call, my counter-offer was to change further the NMCs process and content to suit their needs but I refused to deny participants the opportunity to fully explore themselves, experience new negotiation and leadership skills and challenge the organization.

I understand where the Oil Corp. executives stand, how they likely experienced their negotiators and team members challenging themselves more frequently, how different my NMCs may have seemed and what the executives believed was in their best interests. I admire the executives for the work they do. Overall, they do it very effectively. However, I believe that doing more of what they already do is not the way to achieve their goals for changing their culture and achieving even better negotiated outcomes. I, also, still believe they must be told *no* more often.

Notice the black/white, go/no-go approach they took with the NM Circles. I wanted a fuller debate and negotiation that may have led to differing levels of training for different teams. My judgment that I pronounced at the first meeting—"You dictate and do not negotiate"—seemed accurate. As I stated in my first meeting last December with the six Oil Corp. executives and now again in late August, "No, I will not do that as I believe you will be wasting your money and my time." I had to stand up to the "bully" like behavior of Oil Corp. for myself, for the seventy-five negotiators and for Oil Corp.

I did offer to introduce them to negotiation trainers who provide what Oil Corp. said they wanted. I also provided Oil Corp. with materials to use in their in-house basic training.

Changing Culture Involves Personal Change

It helps to understand that leadership is not a concrete concept, stable over time. Rather, true leadership is fluid, and adapts to needs.
    Jeanne McPherson, Ph.D.

As change agents, while we must take our clients from where they are, we must also "walk our talk." We must not settle for what's comfortable and easy. We must challenge our clients and ourselves. Inciting insurgency to new insights is a strong way to new perspectives and new ways of doing things. As change agents we must be ready to walk away from a contract or deal that we do not believe will help the client achieve their stated objectives. A change agent who believes in challenging and testing everything, cannot do anything without testing and challenging themselves.

In hindsight, I needed to better ensure the Oil Corp.'s executives truly understood the personal changes required to transform their culture. I would have served Oil Corp. better by spending much more time early on to deepen the understanding of (and the negotiation behind) my approaches, expectations, measures of success, accountability and challenges for each of them. Yet with the transfer out of some of the leaders, and in of others, during the program, the commitment I received early on was not honored. I had been true to my position that I will not waste their money and time on tactics and strategies alone. I was bringing the realms of negotiation and the new definition of leadership far stronger into my NM Circle design and communications. I walked away from a deal that served neither of us. I walked away from $75,000. I kept my values and commitments. Several of my peers have told me that I was crazy and should have taken the money. I may be crazy but my values include integrity. What would you do for $75,000? Where is your "No"?

Three years later, I played golf with one of the senior oil sands negotiators at Oil Corp. I asked him what had changed in the way he negotiates within Oil Corp. and with other companies and the government. He said they have very little room to negotiate, the executive team still dictates to them and they are very successful. I asked him how he does within that environment. "I wish I had more authority and ability to influence. But I have been there for over 13 years, they treat me well and it's ok." At dinner, we laughed together. He said, "It really isn't a place you negotiate. We do everything 100 percent and rarely have working interest partners. When you drill 800 wells a year, partners slow you down." My reply: "Few companies can stand working with you guys. It's your way or the highway." "That's true," he confirmed with a laugh.

Life is a negotiation. People judge us more by our qualities and intentions than our proclamations; more in our "being" in negotiations than our "doing." Understanding this leads to trust, respect, positive relationship and sustainable and significant agreements.

If we are to have the talent that we need to be competitive in the future, we must focus on the sustainability of people.

Dee Ann Turner, It's My Pleasure: The Impact of Extraordinary Talent and A Compelling Culture. [73]

While I highly value negotiation, collaboration and conflict resolution skills, Oil Corp. is one of the most successful Canadian companies and they got there and stay there through very tight controls. Their strategy matches how they do business. That is a great lesson.

By the way, when I asked my golfing partner from Oil Corp. how specific executives were doing, he replied most of the six I had negotiated with had either retired or where no longer in the operations area. I wondered how Oil Corp. was dealing with such a significant shift in talent and leadership. He stated that it was challenging for everyone but they were developing a new generation of leaders. These new leaders are promoted on their ability to strategize and adhere to the corporate culture.

You say you've got to win at any cost
No golden rule, no line you haven't crossed
So what if Mother Earth's in tatters
You're the only one that matters
Sorry buddy, you've already lost
I have a dream that there's enough for everyone
And it's not about who's lost and who has won.
It's so simple, it's so wise
No defeat, no compromise
It's the future and it's already begun
It's a brand new game and that's the way we play.
No exceptions no excuses
No one wins if someone loses
Everybody wins or find a better way
We've got to win, win, win or walk away...
So let's choose the very best
And together we'll Break Through to Yes

Chuck Rose, "Win or Walk Away," written and performed for Break Through to Yes: The Radio Show. [74]

The Hidden Costs of Collaboration

All too often plans involving collaboration among different parts of an organization are unveiled with fanfare only to collapse or fizzle out later. The best way to avoid such an outcome is to determine before you launch an initiative whether it is likely to yield a collaboration premium. A collaboration premium is the difference between the projected financial return on a project and two often overlooked factors—opportunity cost and collaboration costs.

It's a mistake to underestimate collaboration costs in the hope that collaboration can be mandated or will naturally improve during the course of a project.

All the team members tried to protect their own customers," one manager in the certification group admitted. Because of the reluctance to share customer relationships, the team had to significantly reduce its estimates of the revenue to be generated by cross-selling.

Individual members of the cross-unit team were also pulled by conflicting goals and incentives. Only one team member was dedicated to the initiative full-time; most people had to meet individual targets within their respective units while also working on the joint project. Some people got a dressing down from their managers if their cross-unit work didn't maximize their own unit's revenue.

Even those who saw the benefits of the initiative found it hard to balance their two roles. "We all had personal agendas," said one senior manager in the certification group. "It was difficult to prioritize the food initiative and to pull people out of their daily work to do the cross-area work.

"When Internal Collaboration Is Bad for Your
Company" by Morten T. Hansen [75]

Blindness

When truly opening up to the ideas of others in collaboration, we have the opportunity to go beyond our own rules and beliefs and explore ideas and possibilities that we alone cannot see or choose not to see.

    Richard Schultz

Too often we don't see what is in front of us. We have been conditioned to see through our own experiences, perspectives and blinders. Our brain cleverly sifts through what it perceives and then presents it to us in a way that aligns with our experiences and expectations. Autism is thought to be a brain without filters. Everything comes through and an autistic person struggles to make sense of it all. The other extreme is people and groups that simply refuse to see anything that doesn't fit their social frame.

Most every leader knows that at times we and our organization have blind spots. For those who don't, go online and find the video of the *Invisible Gorilla* by Christopher Chabris and Daniel Simons. [76]

"Imagine you are asked to watch a short video (above) in which six people—three in white shirts and three in black shirts—pass basketballs around. While you watch, you must keep a silent count of the number of passes made by the people in white shirts. At some point, a gorilla strolls into the middle of the action, faces the camera and thumps its chest, and then leaves, spending nine seconds on screen. Would you see the gorilla?

Almost everyone has the intuition that the answer is, "Yes, of course I would." How could something so obvious go completely unnoticed? But when we did this experiment at Harvard University several years ago, we found that half of the people who watched the video and counted the passes missed the gorilla. It was as though the gorilla was invisible.

This experiment reveals two things: that we are missing a lot of what goes on around us, and that we have no idea that we are missing so much."

We miss so much. We are blind often. Through collaboration and by embracing diversity and conflict, we create conditions that may allow less blindness.

What is the gorilla in the room that you do not see?

Inattentional blindness, also known as perceptual blindness, is a psychological lack of attention and is not associated with any vision defects or deficits. It may be further defined as the event in which an individual fails to recognize an unexpected stimulus that is in plain sight. The term was coined by Arien Mack and Irvin Rock in 1992 and was used as the title of their book of the same name, published by MIT press in 1998] Here, they describe the discovery of inattentional blindness and include a collection of procedures used describing the phenomenon. Research on inattentional blindness suggests that the phenomenon can occur in any individual, independent of cognitive deficits. When it simply becomes impossible for one to attend to all the stimuli in a given situation, a temporary blindness effect can take place as a result; that is, individuals fail to see objects or stimuli that are unexpected and quite often salient.[77]

The Collaboration Meme

Collaboration is hardwired into the human brain and an evolutionary advantage for most species.

Ken Cloke

A meme (/ˈmiːm/meem) is "an idea, behavior, or style that spreads from person to person within a culture." A meme acts as a unit for carrying cultural ideas, symbols, or practices that can be transmitted from one mind to another through writing, speech, gestures, rituals, or other imitable phenomena with a mimicked theme. Supporters of the concept regard memes as cultural analogues to genes in that they self-replicate, mutate, and respond to selective pressures. [78]

With this book and your own networks and experiences, we are building a meme of collaboration and a culture of collaboration. Each walk around The

10 Essential Steps, each walk around the circle learning from failure and each walk around your own organization is an evolutionary step. See yourself as a leader, a meme, carrying practices and ideas to your network and spheres of influence. In some ways, collaboration is a system of continuous development and learning and outreach. Through the meme-like behaviors, we all learn and bring back to the practice and community.

Part Four

Break Through

Collaborative leadership reflects the increasing complexity of
multiple, competing stakeholders in organizational outcomes.
Jeanne McPherson, Ph.D.

Business is increasingly complex and, to some, can't be fully understand-able. The pressure on leaders to be in control serves the opposite. When we want to employ our intelligent and agile team to get things done inside and outside, we move away from the old organization chart that looks like a huge pyramid with the "boss" at the top. Over the past several decades, we have adopted matrix organization structures to respect the reality that the functions employees do and the projects they are involved in have different reporting and networks. What might an organization structured based on holistic, balanced, empowered, networked and agile teams focused on achieving the big value additions look like? I see the old top down organizational chart as flat, the matrix chart as two dimensional and the collaborative organization chart as not only three dimensional but, also, in flow constantly changing.

Here are some insights from Robert L. Cross, Roger D. Martin, and Leigh M. Weiss to better help us understand the management of networks:

As collaboration within and among organizations becomes increasingly important, companies must improve their management of the networks where it typically occurs. Although collaboration is at the heart of modern business processes, most companies are still in the dark about how to manage it. Linear, process-based tools such as activity-based costing, business process reengineering, and total quality management have long been effective at measuring and improving the efficiency of people and organizations in accomplishing individual tasks. But they do a poor job of shedding light on the largely invisible networks that help employees get things done across functional, hierarchical, and business unit boundaries.

This blind spot has become problematic. Falling communications costs, globalization, and the increasing specialization of knowledge-based work have made collaboration within and among organizations more important than ever. As "tacit" interactions replace more routine economic activity and the scale and complexity of many corporations creep upward, the need to manage collaboration is growing. Nearly 80 percent of the senior executives surveyed in a 2005 study said that effective coordination across product, functional, and geographic lines was crucial for growth. Yet only 25 percent of the respondents described their organizations as "effective" at sharing knowledge across boundaries.

Once executives understand the value that's flowing across networks, they can intervene in straightforward, cost-justified ways. Typical examples include replicating high-performing networks, training workers to emulate the collaborative approaches of successful colleagues, making valuable expertise and advice more readily available, and revamping performance metrics to reflect mutual accountabilities better. These kinds of successful interventions can help companies reduce complexity, redefine roles, serve customers and clients more effectively, and allocate financial, physical, and human resources more efficiently. [79]

Business is increasingly complex and, to some, can't be fully understandable. The pressure on leaders to be in control serves the opposite. When we want to employ our intelligent and agile team to get things done inside and outside, we move from the old organization chart that looks like a huge pyramid with the "Boss" at the top. Over the past several decades, we have adopted matrix organization structures to respect the reality that the functions employees do and the projects they are involved in have different reporting and networks. What might an organization structured based on holistic, balance, empowered, networked and agile teams focused on achieving the big value additions look like? I see the old top down org.

chart as flat, the matrix chart as two dimensional and the collaborative organization chart as not only three dimensional but, also, in flow constantly changing.

> To see an inspiring video of the extreme level of collaboration, watch the Mumuration of Starlings videos on Vimeo, YouTube and other sites. Here is a great example of how starling shape shift.[80]

Imagine your organization as one that is flexible, connected and independent. How will you create the conditions for this future potential? Kevin Nuveu, President of Precision Drilling, Calgary, Alberta has a vision:

Highly collaborative organizations provide senior leaders broad and diverse perspectives on the business challenges and usually results in the opportunity to consider a wider range of strategic alternatives to achieve the desired objectives. More importantly, the collaborative organization can improve decision making through a review of a wider range of options and robust discussion and through this process organizational "buy in" and support can be effected much deeper through organization thereby increasing the probability of a successful outcome.

Negotiation and Conflict

Collaboration offers the creative and courageous space to weave the threads that connect, innovate, and lead change for a world of change.
Kerry Woodcock

Sometimes dropping our story, seeing things in new perspectives and gaining courage to let go of positions allow us to break through our barriers.

In mid-2015, Dave Gould, a self-described reformed lawyer and mediator and Co-Founder with me of the Global Negotiation Insight Institute, Calgary, Alberta was called into help resolve a major commercial conflict that had been in litigation for seven years. In a posh downtown Calgary office tower, Dave was seated at the head of a large rectangular boardroom table with the representatives of each of the battling corporations down either side. After the preliminaries, Dave asked, "How long has this legal battle been going on?" "Seven years" was the answer. David asked the combatants to consider the size of this large boardroom and to mentally place in this board room all the boxes of evidence, proceedings and notes that had been filled over seven years. "Would those boxes fill this large room?" The combatants responded that all those boxes would likely fill two boardrooms of this size. Dave let them hold that visual for a few minutes. He then asked whether those two boardrooms of boxes they had filled over seven years had brought them closer to the resolution of their conflict. No reply from either side of the expansive table. He let that thought sink in for a while as well. "So in your own mind, stand up and close and lock the doors to those two rooms of boxes. You keep the key but the rooms are now out of sight and not part of this conversation," led Dave. Counsel for one of the sides spoke up as he noticed some real agitation in the room amongst the executives. "Now this is very unusual and while I have no idea where Mr. Gould is going with this, but I am prepared to play along."

Dave checked with the other lawyer and got a cautious green light then said, "Everything in those two large boardrooms in all of those boxes filled over seven years is simply a story. It is a story that is not serving the best interests of either party here. Now, leave those two rooms locked and let's explore the business relationship that each of you would rather have with the other side than what you have been doing for seven years." Within a few days, the companies negotiated a healthier and more productive business relationship and had settled the case.

Free ourselves from the stories that are not serving us. Dave Gould was offering a spiritual, Buddhist- like process of letting go and letting come. Letting go of the heavy stone that we too often carry in business and personal relationships allows us first to see the interests and aspirations we share then, second, to collaborate to achieve those aspirations.

Be Aware (Step 2) that some may not see their interests and aspirations served. Many litigation lawyers and firms may find this a horror story. I know many very successful lawyers who know their success is by serving the interest and aspirations of their clients.

The Collaboration Circle

Recognizing that everyone has something significant to bring to the project, listening and communicating well, and sharing ideas and resources can create extraordinary results—results that generally far surpass anything that a single individual alone is able to create

Linda Matthie

So much of what we believe is right and common sense does not seem like right or common sense to others. So much of what we believe is right and common sense in our profession and our industry does not seem like right or common sense to others. The stakes for ourselves, our communities, our nation and our world seem to escalate. So much challenge, conflict and change is happening now. We have never been here before. Elders are limited in their guidance to us. Where may we turn for wisdom? Will this decade mean the end of the world as we know it? Yes. Here's why:

Some of my American clients and audiences have challenged me on Dirty Canadian Oil, the Keystone XL Pipeline, shale gas fracturing, the Northern Gateway pipeline and more. At the same time, some of my Canadian clients were challenging me to help them gain or regain their places in the executive suites of organizational power. We also see the massive challenges facing our youth, our aboriginal peoples and our earth experience. There is a way to enlighten these conversations and challenges.

Question: what and whose interests are served by these perceptions of anger and animosity? Might the media sell more from a place of fear and separation than dreams and oneness? Might the politicians? Might the environmentalists? Might the oil industry? Would it be conceivable that the funding for hard-line environmental groups comes from American companies whose interests are served by monopolizing the market for Canadian resources? What is leadership? Where is leadership? Leadership is a scarce resource. Leadership is not ramming your way through obstacles. Leadership is listening and leading. In late 2015, President Obama, killed the Keystone XL Pipeline. By most every measure, that decision was symbolic and branding for the Democratic candidates in 2016. The decision had little to do with environmental protection, climate change or economics. Why do we waste over eight years and hundreds of millions of dollars on planning, review and more, when decisions like these are made too often? [81]

Consider that all the expertise and experience we each have may not be enough to effectively and successfully deal with the great challenges we face today as individuals, families, organizations, professions and nations. Consider the collective wisdom that is possible from a circle of listening, speaking, understanding and co-creating solutions.

This is an invitation to engage with people who care about subjects and questions that matter to you and your organization. Your circle or team will be most successful in solving significant challenges when you bring in others whose opinions and experiences are very different from yours. We can no longer afford "groupthink" or "yes men." The stakes are high. We must invite in the First Nations, the environmentalists, the Americans, the Asians, the youth, the wise women. We must embrace conflict.

These are the principles of great circles;

1.   Our intention must be authentic,

2.   We build relationship and trust first,

3.   We invite and respect diversity of opinion,

4.   We establish key questions that matter,

5.   We listen,

6.   We seek new ideas from the collective wisdom,

7.   We are open to unexpected outcomes,

8.   We take as long as it takes,

9.   We commit to action and hold accountability.

So what are the questions that matter? From our list of significant challenges we face, choose with courage and vision. Remember not to sell or attempt to convince others. Understand what the underlying interests are and be open to what arises.

As leaders, let's work with all the diversity of opinions and perspectives we can. Let's create outcomes never believed possible. And let's move from "Mediot" championed division to an inclusive vision. A wonderful outcome is that business may then do better business and create better bottom lines. We have seen too much of the fear based mentality that only serves select interests.

Circles and teams do not always result in great outcomes. In fact, sometimes they fail if the intention is not honest or when a conflict is feared. The effectiveness of a circle is determined by the quality of the intentions and actions of all the participants. Circles may result in transformative relation-ships and outcomes. That is worth it. That is how the next decade will be very different than prior times. Leaders will lead now with respect, patience, vision, purpose and engagement. Welcome, leader.

When asked why I would take on such a dangerous role, I have clearly stated that there is nothing I know that may be more important for our nation, province, communities, aboriginal nations, earth, economy and future than bringing together leaders to co-create breakthroughs that honor all.

Chief Collaboration Officer

Your integrity and values must be aligned or collaboration fails.
Shawne Duperon.

The greatest advance in organizational productivity in the knowledge economy is the rise of the Chief Collaboration Officer. The CCO is respon-sible for aligning corporate strategy and objectives with the best resources and people inside and outside the organization. More will get accomplished in less time with fewer resources, allowing more projects to get launched and scaled. For the small entrepreneur, having a collaboration expert on your advisory board and/or network will provide necessary innovation and leadership.

Here is a simple and clear position description for the CCO. The CCO is the one who asks and then acts on this question: "Given this intention, who and what are the very best resources available inside and outside our organi-zation that are and will be necessary to accomplish our vision? And what is the best way for us to work together?"

> The leader of the future will be a building of partnerships across, up and down in the com-pany as well as a building of partnerships with suppliers, customers and business partners outside of the company.
> *Marshall Goldsmith.*

Collaboration. It's a $1 billion industry, according to an ABI Research study on worker mobility and enterprise social collaboration. And it's projected to grow to $3.5 billion by 2016.

No wonder lots of ink has been spilled on this business buzzword on everything from how to start (hint: build trust) to doing it better with social platforms, to using it as a way to achieve that holy grail of business: innovation.

Two years ago, the *Harvard Business Review* even touted the need for another C-suite executive: the CCO. A chief collaboration officer would be charged with integrating the enterprise as companies scramble to innovate from within. But in an ideal scenario, this most critical of business strategies would have a dedicated individual toiling to make collaboration part of the daily doings of the company. The CCO would have their place among the top brass. Despite the highly trained focus on the benefits of collaboration, according to Jacob Morgan, a principal of the social media consultancy Chess Media Group and scourer of collaboration practices, there's only one CCO in the U.S. And The Motley Fool has him. Tom Gardner, Motley Fool's cofounder and CEO says that when you're working on a project, the easiest route is often to just do it yourself—but it's not often the best idea.

"You don't have to compromise, you don't have to teach someone, you don't have to deal with other people's timetables," Gardner says. "Doing it yourself works well for the short-term, but it's toxic if you're trying to create a workplace culture that supports learning and employee development." [82]

Alpha and Beta

Dana Ardi, author of *The Fall of the Alphas*, said during an interview with *Business News Daily* that:

For centuries, the hierarchical style and structures that I call the Alpha paradigm was the only way leaders led, and the only way organizations organized. As I explain in *The Fall of the Alphas*, leaders asserted themselves aggressively, competed rather than collaborated, and conquered rather than compromised. This trickled down to younger generations as the single template of how to be, act, behave, and aspire.

Organizations were constructed like pyramids with predetermined and narrowly defined steps or rungs leading to the top. The slightest suggestion of a more community-oriented or compassionate approach was seen as "soft," certainly not sufficient to lead a "tough" organization through "tough" times.

But everything changed with the dawn of the Informational Age. It was my realization that work in the Information Age is heuristic— it stimulates inquiry, trial and error and is fluid. Creativity, technology, social change and globalization have created the opportunity to rethink how we organize and come together. The new Beta way is all about the way we need to connect, collaborate, and influence to meet the challenges of this information age

Beta companies have disadvantages if poorly implemented. Many leaders feel loss of control. Many employees, if not properly considered and self-motivated, feel role confusion. Coordination and organizational learning must occur or there will be confusion. Beta organizational principles are not suitable for all activities but collaboration and open communication is still a Beta cultural imperative. Beta organizations must evolve. Their success relies on self-awareness and personal responsibility." [83]

Our Hope/Our Commitment

I can't help but have compassion and understanding for you, the leadership, who have pressures beyond our awareness. But if our collaboration means we agree to agree with you for the sake of convenience, well count me out. The truth is we want change and success in our working together but our varying agendas and fears keep us apart, we need to be humble enough to allow the presence of everyone to be part of the solution, not just in words and good feelings but in actions and behaviors.

Robin Wesman, spiritual businessman, Jaffray, British Columbia

Together, we have explored collaboration from "why" stories, what is needed, failures, experiences, shared wisdom, a step-by-step process and much more. We titled this book *Break Through to Yes: Unlocking the Possible within a*

Culture of Collaboration. I sincerely hope you and your organization will make many breakthroughs by effectively leading and creating a culture of collaboration.

To make it easier on yourself and those around you, expect failures, frustrations and roadblocks. But effective collaboration takes time. Building a collaborative culture takes far more time.

Look at all of this as a path forward or a spiral upward. There will be times when you get burned or lose key people. There will be times when you are alone. And there will be a growing recognition that you are by your actions and your spirit a true leader.

"The most important and basic principal to follow is the Golden Rule. When we have a mutual relationship based on respect, trust, hard work, intelligence, skill and mutual gain, we will have a long term and successful relationship," *Robert G. Peters, President of Black Diamond Land & Cattle Co. and Founder of Peter's & Co., Calgary, Alberta.*

In the last two quotes, compare the wisdom of a spiritual businessman in a village in British Columbia with that of one of the wealthiest and most respected businessmen in Canada. The mutual gain, respect and trust are at the heart of both.

As the world gets smaller and smaller through economic, communications and travel advances, leaders are becoming far more successful when they include, dream, act and serve with and for others. When we develop our personal and business network globally with people with whom we have a "mutual relationship based on respect, trust, hard work, intelligence, skill and mutual gain," we are far better working together.

"I think everything that's happening today in the form of protest whether it's occupy Wall Street or the Arab Spring or the environmental movement or watershed protection specific to our case, the ultimate issue globally is that people want to be heard. They feel like they are disconnected from the decision-making process and we are going to hear about it and hear about it until something's done. It's not necessarily the people making the decisions who are at fault. There seems to be a systemic failure going on where people cannot get their word across. There's a definite disconnect between what the voter wants, what the public wants and what is happening at the decision making level and, to me, whether it's what I do on the watershed protection site or whether it's financial issues or other political areas or democracy, it needs to change. It has to change. Whether it's people protesting in the streets or some way to improve the way democracy is being utilized, I think this is going to be a defining issue over the next five, six years to a decade," *Glenn Isaac.*

By reading this book, challenging GroupThink, inviting others in and developing the collaborative culture in your organization, you are at the forefront of this change. Organizations on this path have a strategic advantage over others who stick to the "command and control" or "us versus them" organizations. This does take time and as you get better, your organization will be more respected, intelligent, agile and successful.

Make It So.

We stand together in this natural space. We are up to 150 years old. We are young. We have tiny wild flowers and moss at our feet. We have a wetland as our close neighbor. We have deer, elk, bear, moose, cougar, ants, worms, gray jays, osprey, bald eagles, loons, bats, painted turtles, squirrels, caterpillars and lichen. We are alive. We are healthy. We are green. The air is fresh. We are Tamarack, Ponderosa Pine, Fir and Birch. With our neighbors, we are an ecosystem. Together, we are a forest. We provide everything we need. We depend on one another and this ecosystem. We work together well.

We are coming together in new ways as we begin to Break Through to Yes by unlocking possibilities from within a culture of collaboration.

Appendix A

About the Author

David is founder and President of Savage Management Ltd., Think Sustain Ability Consultants and The Collaborative Global Initiative.

Savage Management Ltd. (founded in 1993) provides consulting, negotiation, conflict management, organizational development, stakeholder engagement, coaching and collaborative leadership services. www.savagemanage.com.

The Collaborative Global Initiative (founded in 2013) is a global community of collaborative and dispute resolution professionals, located in Canada, the United States, Spain, the Netherlands and Ecuador. CGI is committed to addressing and embracing conflict, and supporting a more peaceable, healthy and sustainable living environment in families, communities, business and our world.

Clients include executives and organizations involved in oil and gas, aboriginal development, conflict management, community, renewable energy, law, resort management, not-for-profits and primary health care. Savage's clients are organizations that have strong leadership committed to actively developing their people and their objectives by positive leadership, collaboration, stakeholder engagement, conflict management and business development. Our clients have real and current challenges within and without their organizations that are adversely affecting attainment of their objectives.

David is, also, a cofounder of the Company to Company Dispute Resolution Council, the Alberta Energy Regulator Dispute Resolution Program, the Global Negotiation Insight Institute and Synergy Alberta.

Between 1975 and 2007, David held executive positions with Sebring Energy, TriQuest Energy, BXL Energy, Westar Petroleum, Total Petroleum and Ashland Oil. David, also, served as Chair of the Calgary Chamber of Commerce Dispute Resolution Committee, Director of the Small Explorers and Producers Association of Canada, President of the Petroleum Joint Venture Association and the Canadian Association of Petroleum Producers Alberta Executive Policy Group. He has served on many committees of the Canadian Association of Petroleum Landmen over the past 40 years.

After a successful thirty-two-year career as a leader in the Canadian petroleum industry, since 2007 David has focused on engaging and developing collaborative leaders and sustainable business development.

David's current volunteer board positions include ʔaqʼam (St. Mary's Indian Band) Community Enterprises (part of the Ktunaxa First Nation of BC) and the Heart and Stroke Foundation Alberta and NWT. David, also, is an active volunteer for the TransCanada Trail, TrailsBC, Rotary and the Canadian Association of Professional Speakers.

David's co-shared book, *Ready Aim Excel: 52 Leadership Lessons*, is an international business bestseller on Amazon. David, also, hosts a weekly business radio show on Voice America; Break Through to Yes with Collaboration. The podcasts of all the episodes of the show are available on iTunes.

Appendix B
Wisdom from My Advisers on Why Collaborate:

Alissa Amos/Teacher/Daughter, British Columbia; "To learn."

Amy Fox/Organizational Development, Massachusetts: "You stretch yourself as a practitioner both because you learn from other's gifts and skills, but also because it pulls out other qualities from your own practice to work next to other talented professionals."

Bryce Medd/Wealthy Tortoise Financial, British Columbia: "In the financial services realm, if the intention is to create one plan, a road map for a client, then only by collaboration can all of the various disciplines come together for the best interest of the client—the only thing that should be considered."

Carley Knutson/Alberta: "Brain storming. My favorite thing to do is sit down with people from differing viewpoints and step outside a puzzle and see what gets created by the building of ideas."

Carrie Schafer/Publisher, British Columbia: "I believe the number-one reason to collaborate is to build a better sector/community/region together. When regional groups get together for funding purposes it makes it easier on the funder to support the proposal as they see the groups working together for the betterment of the region, community or sector. By collaborating, groups have access to shared expertise, resources, and can partner to save money and strengthen the sector."

Cinnie Noble/Ontario: "To harness the potential within and for all those who come together to attain and optimize their shared purpose in a mutually satisfactory way."

Colin Campbell/British Columbia: "The definition 'to work jointly on an activity to produce or create something' does not imply that collaborating is a partnership or a business venture but rather an intellectual adventure to create something such as a paper or to work on a specific subject. It could be something that needs dealing with and by putting a number of individuals together to work on the project a solution is developed that will benefit the greater good."

Dr. Hedy Bach/Professor, Alberta: "Increase connections between ideas/knowledge that can lead to creative/active/innovative possibilities."

Dr. Nancy Love/Alberta: "Reasons for collaborating are not always evident to someone who has spent most of their lives trying to be right or feeling like they need to be expert at something. The collaborative processes seem cumbersome and time consuming especially when you are *sure* you know what needs to happen. In my experience the process is when the learning occurs for people. Throughout the collaborative process they begin to understand the value of the dialogue that brings people together and creates a *team* before the project even begins. Relationships forged in collaborative processes are strong and respectful. You know where someone is coming from once you have been in a collaborative process with them. You know how to meet their needs and to express your own needs in a way that they can hear you. The outcome of a collaboration may be the same as it would have been if one person had made the decision. But the results are different. There is buy-in and on-boarding and engagement as fall out and that is worth its weight and the time you spend. It is an investment that helps you avoid resistance down the line. You know...the resistance that contributes to projects being over budget and over time."

"How a decision is made is as important as what the decision is. Collaborate early and often for successful projects."

Garth Wiggill/British Columbia and South Africa: "Minimize conflict (in other words, piss off as few people as possible)."

Heather Savage/Manager, Toronto Ontario: "People should check their subjectivity, be aware of their assumptions and interpretations, as well as privileges when offering advice. It's the stuff that can make collaborative work really rich, but also really alienate people and exclude people."

Jan Boydol/Consultant/Alberta: "When you lead from the heart instead of the head, you are naturally in a collaborate state of mind and emitting heart energy. That heart energy becomes contagious to those people with whom you are dealing, be they work associates, business associates, fellow board members, family members, friends, and adversaries. Collaborations are most successful when it starts in the heart energy before head energy joins in.

Shifting thought from a control and command paradigm to a collaborative approach depends on establishing a successful communication pathway between heart/head/the two different hemispheres of the brain via the corpus collosum, which is the linking pathway between the two hemispheres. (In itself a collaboration)."

Jason Donev/Professor, Alberta: "We benefit from the perspective and expertise of others."

John Griffith/Alberta: "The presence of other equal partners with different perspectives helps to discipline my ego (preconceived solutions and easy answers) and calls forth my gifts to contribute toward a solution that is bigger than I could have imagined."

Krystal Oleson/Consultant/British Columbia: "With shared ideas, perspectives and knowledge it is possible to create well-rounded and appropriate processes in order to meet a need or a goal."

Maxine Morrison/Alberta: "The art of collaboration is when a common goal comes to fruition by exchange of ideas, insights and knowledge being shared by two or more people. Most collaboration requires leadership to keep a focused discussion with the task or goal top of mind. The concept of brainstorming really is the heart of collaboration that has the potential to give infinite resources. Collaboration is not always easy, with more people comes more variety of insights and different ideas on how to get to the same goal. Making decisions for the best outcome can prove difficult, for even the best leaders. However, when it comes together it is a beautiful thing, which is why collaboration is a form of art!"

Michelle Phaneuf/Conflict Resolution, Alberta "Collaboration brings great minds together and creates outcomes that will surpass your wildest dreams. It's also a lot more fun to work together with totally different minds and create something you could never have thought of in isolation."

Rick Hatala, BSC, P.Eng, PMP/Organizational Development, Alberta: "To co-create a product, service or result that you could not do as well alone."

Ron Salt/Oil Industry, Alberta: "To learn what each party values to identify the best win-win outcome."

Scott Meakin/Oil Industry, Alberta: "Because it feels good (life really should be hedonistic). The energy derived out of successfully collaborating can't be beat. Not only do you get to experience success but the feeling of team and self is significantly enhanced. It fosters appreciation for diversity of thought and wisdom and though I don't have any clinical proof I'm sure you get an endorphin boost."

Shawne Duperon/Michigan: "It's the only way to create real influence and expand. Real leaders never get anywhere on their own. We tap into the momentum of other leaders with similar visions, to cause global shifts."

Sherry Matheson/Alberta: "Collaboration is a great way for a team to learn, grow and be innovative. Helps members learn how to relate to each other and how to make decisions with all the different perspectives. Requires each of the individuals on the team to learn, grow and develop their skills, which is beneficial to collaborating as a team."

Stephen Hobbs (DrWELLth)/Alberta: "You collaborate to move individual achievement through the efforts of others to realize collective accomplishment. One can do things to a level of realization that is helpful to self for others = achievement = performance. Then, there are other things best served through collaborative effort that realize an expansive level of realization of some for others = accomplishment = productivity. When you collaborate, it is a dynamic balance of assertiveness of self and cooperation with others = a balance of performative achievement and productive accomplishment."

Susan Brady/Organizational Development, Massachusetts: "Better output (more creative, innovative, useful)."

Tina Spiegel/Australia: "The reason to use Collaboration as a process is because it holds key elements which we, as relational beings (I borrow the term from Kenneth J. Gergen, *Relational Being Beyond Self and Community*) treasure. We are relational beings and all things flow from relationship."

Trish Barnes/Communications, British Columbia: "Faith: 'Together, we can create excellence!'"

Viki Winterton/Publisher, New Mexico: "As world-wide business becomes the norm, joining forces and combining resources is one of the most critical paths to success in our global environment."

Robin Oaks/Mediator, California: "The word 'collaborative' drew me because I am alone and I can resonate with that sense of what I feel wealth of wisdom that has been developing in my life path and yet I'm alone and I know there's a box around my thinking and my way of connecting. I welcome the opportunity to see where I fit, what I can contribute. There is the connection with others—when people make comments—percolates more out of me and I grow in that. It is in that connection that the change and the growth and the evolution happens but it's got to be in connection. We are connected."

Appendix C
Roadblocks to Collaboration

When I received advice from 100 peers in five nations, a key question I asked (and the question that received the most responses) is "What is the number one reason that collaboration fails?" As you read the responses, consider what is needed to turn a negative into a positive.

Ego:

Alissa Amos—Egos

Amy Fox—Ego. If I spend my time comparing and contrasting my gifts and skills to the person I am working with and going either one up or one down to them I miss the abundance of the situation and the opportunity to ignite and stretch each other to greater heights.

Brad Clarke—Ego

Herky Cutler—Pride/Ego - When one or more members let their pride/ego get in the way of trying new things, being open to new ideas and/or accepting that what has worked in the past may not work any longer, that's usually when collaboration fails.

Michelle Phaneuf, P.Eng C.Med—Egos and fears often get in the way during the collaboration process. My inside voice is always popping up and asking, "Are you sure you are getting as much as the other person?" I have learned to ignore it and work towards an open outcome—which usually get us both more than we thought possible.

Self Interest:

Andrew J. McQuiston—Lack of "buy-in" from one or more of the participants.

Bernie Fitterer—Collaboration fails because individuals are more focused on their vested interests or what is in it for themselves than a greater good. Sadly, when individuals focus exclusively on self-interest, the outcome is less than it can be.

Kevin Barg—Pride, Selfishness, Greed, Immaturity, Ignorance, Lack of Knowledge, Lack of Desire for Knowledge (many of these are related to each other and can be either a root issue or a surface issue).

Lee Wahl—Only worried about your own interests versus joint.

Lynda MacNeill—Personal agendas or objectives.

Mary Ellen & Lorraine Richmond—When the ego or pride is too attached to a particular portion of the process or outcome. When an individual or group of individuals begin to act in a hording manner, rather than with the spirit of generosity for the greater benefit of all, collaboration is awkward and can cease to be productive. Working, thinking and creating together is a discipline of generosity in time, energy and skills.

Rick Hatala, BSc, P.Eng, PMP—Self-interest grounded in fear and a sense of separation.

Competition:

Carrie Shafer—Competition: community groups compete for funding while business compete for business. Lack of Trust - Change in partner manager or unsuitable personality. One or more groups not wanting to let go of control. Lack or loss of a champion.

Cinnie Noble - Competitive behaviors, poor communications, lack of commitment to or sharing the purpose, internal conflict that remains unresolved, lack of a sense of belonging, lack of motivation, cynical, pessimistic, lack of trust, historical experiences that preclude positive and active participation.

Jeffrey M. Cohen, Esq - Collaboration fails when individuals refuse to subordinate their self-interests to the collective consciousness of the group. Refusal to give up one's "turf" is counterproductive to achieving a group's shared vision.

Lack of Trust:

Colin Campbell—Lack of trust. A desire on the part of the politicians to be first or to make a profit over the expense of the other guy. Partnerships in business seldom work and I think it is because the partnership is often formed for economic reasons and the parties being individuals who tend to get things done don't know how to collaborate with someone else.

Dr. Nancy Love—Collaboration fails when the trust in each other is marred by past or present actions, perceived or real, that do not allow the collaborators to be honest with each other. It is vital in business, as it is with astronauts in space, that everyone say what they are thinking. That is the only path to sustainable decisions. When people do not SHARE everything they are thinking or concerned about then the collaboration is based on false information and false relationships. If it is not grounded in open and honest dialog then it can go very wrong. First-time collaborators have not developed a trust in the process to create the best decisions. We know the process allows the kind of input and caution to create not only sustainable but regenerative relationships and GOOD decisions but until someone has seen that happen there is skepticism and concern. I have found two kinds of concerns. There is the "BUT I'm the expert..." concern and there is the "Why should I help them..." concern. Either will get in the way of the deliberately gentle, honest, open and specific talk necessary to ensure results and success from collaboration.

Garth Wiggill—Trust

Henry Mead—The collaboration is not genuinely open to new ideas, and the element of trust is missing.

Pat Van Hesteren—Trust is required to insure that both parties' interests are being addressed and that information shared works to advance all involved. If it is a take-take approach then the collaborative efforts will be for none. Also the inability to express an idea or thought in the way that it was intended can lead to misinterpretation and break down the process. Clarity is critical.

Sherry Matheson—Members of the team not feeling free to express their thoughts, feelings and make mistakes.

Ron Salt—One or more of the participating parties isn't trusted and wants more than their fair share.

Lack of Clarity:

Douglas Stone—Because people are different or they are not good at communicating or aren't clear on their purposes at the outset, or unexpected stress sets in and each person has a different way of coping with it—similar to a marriage.

Susan Brady—Lack of clarity around decision-making/who does what.

No Agreement:

Geoff Greenwell—Lack of solid written agreements. People make the mistake of verbalizing commitments without documenting them and having both (all) parties sign.

Too Hurried:

Gary Ockenden—Not enough conversation before intention formed.

Iris English—When we get into a "me first!" mindset; when we take the way of grabbing the first "right" answer, of not thinking through to outcomes that benefit ALL of the "us," rather than just the singular "us"; when we think only with our wallets, and not with our hearts and logic and ethics; when we fail to listen so that we hear what is being said—and not said; when we choose to feel that anything we want/need is, by definition, more important that what anyone else might want/need; when we fall into the mindset that if "they" get something, it will mean "I" get less...; when we forget that generosity of action and spirit always pays dividends. Maybe that is all summarized by the word "greed"?

Expectations Not Shared:

James Heilman—A lack of a truly shared goal.

Jason Donev—Unreasonable expectations around everyone being on the same page; people often don't have the same goals, methods, values and desired outcomes.

Janice Sommerfeld—Lack of honest, open communication; unequal efforts and/or benefits.

Jodie Kekula—One party is not personally vested in an outcome.

Justin Brown—When there is no defined set of goals or a solid agenda.

Stakeholders Excluded:

James Muraro—Lack of integration or contribution of all individuals in the community.

Incomplete Authority:

Paul Blakeney—Poorly defined decision-making authority. Are we really collaborating, does someone (usually a government, board or legislation) have a trump or impede our work together? The wrong people in the room. Inability or unwillingness to add, exclude/excuse or modify those people in the room overtime as the collaboration moves forward and interest are more fully understood. Choosing to collaborate when another process is more appropriate (arbitration, conciliation/shuttle mediation, authoritative decision making, do nothing, positional bargaining etc.).

Various:

Kristine Skogg—Not listening effectively and/or having the ability to vocalise effectively.

Nick Rubidge—Inequality between partners, or unequal sharing of benefits.

Pete Cheesbrough—Finding the right balance between staying open minded to everything, and sticking to what one believes is right. Compromising with other people's views and perspectives in service of a desired outcome requires humility, confidence and faith.

Peter K. Hisch—Failure to plan, and communicate the plan on how we will collaborate efforts.

Philip H. Shecter, P.C.—Someone, whether a party participant or professional creating a split between the parties and creating entrenchment with certain positions; usually occurs when one or more professionals in the process either fails to develop necessary skills or allows him or herself to align with one party's position instead of encouraging remaining open to discussion of all possible outcomes.

Ray MacEachern—Participant(s)'s unwillingness to compromise.

Richard Schultz—My sense is that collaboration fails when there is a "misalignment" of the purpose, vision and values driving the collaboration. When there is clarity and agreement of these fundamental factors, then the probability of success improves. These become guiding principles to focus intention toward an outcome.

Scott Meakin—Lack of alignment with line of sight to agreed objectives or goals. If there isn't a clear line of site between the project's objectives and the organization's strategic objectives, then even in the event of apparent success of a project it won't have lasting impact as the project will fall by the wayside for not providing the necessary value add and link to strategic line of sight. Think of this as producing a better loaf of bread when the company's business is only donuts.

Shawne Duperon—When your integrity and values are not aligned. When you have different goals, ideas and values, you clash and you can't deeply cause something. Collaboration requires authentic transparency. One of those transparencies includes a clear idea of who you collaborate with and why. The "how" naturally takes care of itself. Deep collaborators become aligned.

Stephen Hobbs (DrWELLth)—Being out of balance between assertiveness and cooperation. Too much assertiveness, slip towards conflicted challenges with others. Too much cooperation, slip towards compromised settlement for you. To collaborate you cannot have assertiveness without cooperation and cooperation without assertiveness. In other words, to have assertiveness you need cooperation and to have cooperation you need assertiveness.

Trish Barnes—Frustration: "Hell is other people!"

Viki Winterton—It must be a win-win.

Dr. Hedy Bach—distorted sense of altruism.

Keith Laws—The drive of humans to attempt to control their environment.

Ken Cloke—

- Neglecting to involve those who are most immediately impacted by the problem
- Not making collaborative improvements in the design of systems, processes, relationships, communications, and technology
- Not reducing or eliminating bureaucratic work that takes time and energy from collaboration efforts
- Inability to visualize what collaboration is intended to achieve, or using it to pursue unclear priorities or vague objectives
- Lack of clarity about how to put it into practice
- Failing to transform existing cultures, processes, and relationships, and significantly alter day-to-day behaviors

Appendix D

Lessons Learned

H ere is a list of a number of collaborative engagement start-ups in which I have been a co-founder and/or leader that did not attain the success I had hoped. Alongside are some of the lessons learned that I incorporate going forward. *Note*: In trying to keep this snapshot short and effective, I do not give full value for the detail and barriers. Most of these have been described elsewhere in this book. Other association and charity work is not shown as I was not a central force. I want you to consider these experiences and what your advice and responses might be.

1.   Collaboration/ Start Date/Additional Leaders

   Global Negotiation Insight Institute
      2008 Erica A. Fox, David Gould, Emily Gould, Ken Cloke, Ron Supancic, Tina Spiegel, Ann Begler, Duncan Autrey, Rachel Wohl, Tony O'Gorman, Lee Jay Berman and others.

   What It Tried To Achieve/Barrier:
   • To bring awareness and skill development for negotiations with other organizations, within our organizations and with ourselves.

   • Was used to promote Erica A. Fox and her wisdom. She left when she focused on the publication of *Winning from Within*. Others were active in Mediators Beyond Borders and the Collaborative Global Initiative.

   What Was Learned/Next Steps:
   While we created GNII to focus on Erica A. Fox and her wisdom,

I felt that was too narrow for the group. I enjoyed the international community that we created and the workshops that we hosted in the USA and Canada. I am friends with many of the people I met through the Global Negotiation Insight Institute. G.N.I.I. has since died. To host, learn from and grow that international network, I co-founded the Collaborative Global Initiative.

2.   TrailsBC

1990s (me since 2008), Al Skucas, Leon Lebrun, Neil Shuttleworth and others.

What It Tried To Achieve/Barrier:
- To develop, maintain and promote non-motorized trail development across British Columbia with connections to the TransCanada Trail.
- Too few people prepared to commit so much over so many years for the region's benefit.

What Was Learned/Next Steps:
- With national dreams/visions and national and provincial/state stakeholders and gatekeepers, often those same organizations are the greatest obstacle. Their regulatory, legal and policies make it very challenging for the local leaders and "do-ers" to accomplish the goal. There is a dichotomy/friction between Step 8, "Collaborate with Vision" and Step 9, "Now Lead" and Step 10, "Make It So."

3.   Rockyview Rural Plan

2010 Sheldon Isaman and others.

What It Tried To Achieve/Barrier:
- To rethink rural subdivision and engage community leaders in a new residential and business community.
- Those in power refused to publicly change their positions while privately they were on our side.

What Was Learned/ Next Steps:

- A more in-depth assessment process in advance of the start of this collaborative effort. The process provided great input and relationship building. The property developer spent millions over eight plus years with numerous attempts to create a rural subdivision that served the needs and wants of the area and those wishing to move to the area. The approval process was hampered by prior positions, lack of understanding of what the project had become (i.e., one of the greenest rural subdivision plans in Canada), an unfamiliarity of this type of project by the regional land planners and failure to engage with the gatekeepers due to rules that limit communications and influence by proponents/lobbyists. Seven months of public engagement and a significantly revised proposal where summarized in a ten-page report that was not allowed to be given to the decision making board members until the start of the ten minutes allowed for the review of the application on the very full agenda. This process must be changed. And "Be Aware" (Step 2) that public figures, at times, have very different conversations in private than the positions they proclaim in public. Your collaborative design is critical.

Like many of these initiatives, how will you decide on what to get involved in and what to avoid or fight? Your decision can't be based on popularity and probability of success. It should be based on your values, skills, resources and vision. How would you decide? I recommend you develop a decision matrix for yourself and for your organization or team. How will we decide is a critical pre-collaboration tool?

4. Columbia Valley Recreation Access Council

2011 Gerry Wilkie, Peter Holmes, Pat Morrow, Lyle Wilson, Juri Peepre, Katherine Hamilton, Craig Paskin and others.

What It Tried To Achieve/Barrier:
- To bring together many conflicting stakeholder/interest groups using public lands in the Columbia Valley to develop understandings, agreements and recommendations to the province on recreational land access and use.

- Motorized interests had a more effective resource in the pro-ATV, truck elected official. Government undermined the process.

What Was Learned/Next Steps:

- Similarly to the Rockyview initiative, "Be Aware" (Step 2) is critical to minimizing wasted time and other resources. While we made good headway and there was a common threat (increasing damage to the environment), the BATNA drove us to stop for some time. In negotiation theory, you are well advised to prepare for your negotiation by considering your best alternative to a negotiated agreement (BATNA) and your worst alternative (WATNA). In the case of the CVRA Council that I was facilitating, the WATNA was that to do nothing could mean the government will resolve it for you or everyone loses because the recreational lands and forest are trashed and no longer serve any groups interests. The motorized groups BATNA was to pull out of the multi-stakeholder group since the Province of British Columbia was not prepared to put any of its strained resources to Land Use Plans at that time and the local Member of the Legislative Assembly for BC was an avid ATV/motorized back country guy who saw those groups as the ones who elected him. The circle game then completed when the provincial authorities said that since the non-motorized groups were not participating, then the CVRAC collaboration was not a credible group.

- What we learned in addition to "Be Aware" is that people change, leaders change and the reasons gatekeepers make decisions change. Three years later Gerry Wilkie and our group are talking about reactivating. The reason is that the Province is more clearly seeing that difficult decisions are increasingly necessary to protect the degradation of the forests, grasslands and riparian areas. And multi-stakeholder groups like CVRAC make those difficult decisions easier. Resources increasingly being spent on compliance and enforcement may be reduced with multi-stakeholder agreements and education.

5. Collaborative Global Initiative

    2013 Duncan Autrey, Jeffrey Cohen, Kathy Porter, Doreen Liberto, Sarah Daitch, Ron Supancic, Christine Calihoo and others.

What It Tried To Achieve/Barrier:

- To create a global community of practice and then a "for-profit" entity for those that choose collaboration, negotiation and dispute resolution as central skills and opportunities for present organizations and our future world. Kathy Porter writes:

I recognize that the conflict often occurs when the "what" is presented before the "why." In other words, someone has decided on the solution but has not offered the opportunity for an informed discussion on why. Another way to consider the CGI (Collaborative Global Initiative) opportunity is from a risk perspective. One party (engineer, government agent) believes risk is something that can be managed to prevent harm verses the other party (general public, activists) believes risk is too high for the harm to be effectively managed. I think there is an opportunity for CGI to focus on challenges of understanding risk in public consultation, mediation and negotiation with a focus on things occurring in a particular 'place.' I believe this based on my experience working on transportation, health care, water treatment and access issues. I think that by grounding our work in something tangible rather than something intangible such as leadership we will make more tracks. The main reason for my thinking this way is that many people already see themselves as leaders and believe they are already collaborating so signing on is more difficult. The leaders will arise through the process. In order to unlock that CGI client door, we need to collaborate amongst ourselves, which is the driving force for me being here.

- Disconnect between what we dream for our world and how we can do it without putting ourselves in financial peril. Like Think Sustain Ability, we are creating a market rather than serving a developed market. Rather, the need is there but the understanding of what collaboration and collaborative leadership is not.

What Was Learned/Next Steps:

- While we found it easy to interest people from around the globe in the possibilities of CGI, we have struggled in:

  a. Creating and communicating a concise, clear and strong value statement; and

  b. Having people consistently contribute their time when they are already very busy in their own work. Most love the possibility of doing this work with this team but until   there are significant net revenues, we can't make the jump. Without the jump, no CGI.

- CGI has very talented professionals from the USA, Canada, Argentina, France and Australia. We have reduced the number of founders from a total of 15 to an active six to create the foundation. We will then return back to the greater group for collaboration. A key aspect of "Design the Collaboration" (Step 5) is to restrict the number of cooks to a small, passionate, intelligent and critical group in the early days. Too many cooks spoil the broth. Or to use another axiom, a camel is a horse designed by a committee.

3. Centre of Excellence in Collaborative Leadership and Change Management

2015 Laura Hummelle and Becky Pelkonen

What It Tried To Achieve/Barrier:
- To engage, educate, link, build resource networks and facilitate the achievement of multi-organizational priorities.

- Leaders use but have limited understanding of collaboration.

What Was Learned/ Next Steps:
- When you pitch and create with very small groups of leaders, you get far more commitment and intelligence than when you go with a larger group. In the Cranbrook and Kimberley area of British Columbia, we were building the initiative. When we brought everyone together to envision, collaborate and design together, politics and smaller thinking took the stage.

- Don't allow those that don't buy-in today to stop you. They may be your biggest champions later. With the world so connected, our collaborations are often most successful wherever you find your community. Today that community may be a collaboration of people in many countries rather than your geographic home. Your niche may attract, serve and profit with 1% of the people in your city and in the world. In Princeton, BC that may be 50 people. In New York City that may be 84,000. In the United States and Canada that may be 3,600,000. In the world, that may be 73,000,000. My point is that by designing a collaboration globally and making the niche or focus very tight, we must keep our group to a few By designing the collaboration and searching very specifically, you will readily find all the participants that you require. While the current generation of gatekeeper's/decision makers (i.e., they are not necessarily leaders or innovators) may not appreciate what you offer, you are the seeds for the future and the world is now your sandbox.

Acknowledgments

To you, the reader, who is taking an active part of this paradigm shift from top down to collaborative leadership; from silo-ed pyramids to evolutionary circles.

To the courageous outliers of the world who choose to positively serve in their own unique ways with their own special skills and perspectives.

To those that stand up for what they believe is right, for innovation and against weak or destructive leaders.

To those who understand that the most rewarding business strategy is one that builds a culture of collaboration that serves community, environment and business.

To the 140 plus people around the world that have provided me with their wisdom for this book and my Internet radio show. Your names are on the inside of the front and back covers. You have made this work a network, intelligent, diverse and inclusive.

To Rhoda Schultz and Krystal Oleson for improving what I do.

To Chuck Rose for writing, recording and sharing the two beautiful theme songs for Break Through To Yes, Win or Walk Away and We Are One.

To all of the hundreds of wonderful leaders who have so freely dedicated themselves to initiatives that I have co-founded, or been an original member of, including;

The Collaborative Global Initiative,

The Centre of Excellence in Collaborative Leadership and Change Management,

Think Sustain Ability,

The Kootenay Leadership Institute,

ʔaqʼam Community Enterprises,

The Global Negotiation Insight Institute,

Synergy Alberta,

The Alberta Energy Regulator Appropriate Dispute Resolution Program,

The Company to Company ADR Council,

Mediators Beyond Borders,

The Professional Enneagram Association of Canada, and

The Calgary Chamber of Commerce ADR Committee.

To Donna Hastings, Rod McKay, Art Korpach, Michael Hill and all the incredible people I work with for the Heart and Stroke Foundation.

To Donna Hastings for seeing the EGOS to be shadowed on my book cover. EGO is the shadow that blocks the light of collaboration.

To Al Skucas, TrailsBC, TransCanada Trail and groups across the world for creating non-motorized trails.

To Rotary International, Cranbrook Sunrise Rotary and to all volunteers in the world, whatever your group and work, that put service above self and make our world better.

To the men and women in the Canadian petroleum industry and the renewable energy industry who do great work through collaboration to provide low price, organic, gluten free energy to consumers across North America.

To Bruce McIntyre, Don Simmons, Harley Hotchkiss, Joan Goldsmith, Graham Woolgar, Linda Matthie, Pat Forest, Wieland Wettstein, Ken Cloke, Colin Campbell, Steve Speer, Donna Hastings, Patricia Morgan, Dale Fisher, Noel Rea, Jim MacLean, Sue Riddell Rose, Rob Peters, Peter Dolezal, Irene Herremans, Iris English, Jimmy Pattison, Margaret Wheatley, Gerry Wilkie, Ron and Monelle Fraser, Judge John Reilly, Karen Dowling, Denise Chartrand, my father Gordon Savage and so many others who have shown me that leadership based on integrity, respect, dedication, inclusion and vision is true leadership in business.

To all my failures, for teaching me.

To the great team at Elevate Publishing, including Mark Russell, AnnaMarie McHargue, Bobby Kuber, Dave Troesh, Emily Border, Jami McNear and Todd Carmen, and to Don Loney, Loney Publishing Group, for taking a 600 plus page draft and turning it into a manuscript, platform and network that will serve my readers and me powerfully. Elevate Savage! You understand, you challenge and your love; thank you. I attended many writers' conferences and interviewed many publishers. I chose you because I trusted you and saw your full spectrum hybrid publishing company as the way to make this book powerfully serve leaders around the world. You have done exactly that. To AnnaMarie McHargue for knowing.

To my grandchildren Quinn and Sara Amos and Bailey and Charlie Rosehill and all the grandchildren and great grandchildren to come. You are the reason.

To my wife, Lise Levesque, for standing with me no matter what. I love you, forever and always! I fell deeply in love with you so easily, we challenge one another, we have one another's back and we give each other freedom to pursue our own passions. Our time from now through 100 will be wonder-filled.

To my children Alissa Amos, Heather Savage and Dan Savage who share a unique heart and soul bond with me and teach me often. To Claire Rosehill and Patrick Gall for embracing me in your world. To Steven Amos, Jamie Henn, Tyler Rosehill and Nicole Weitzel for being there for our children and family. To Carol Todd, my sister, and Todd Girbav, my nephew, for being strong. To my sisters and brothers in our Savage and Levesque families across North America, their partners, children and grandchildren for challenging, encouraging and showing me. To my parents, May and Gordon Savage, for your love and boundaries.

To our beautiful planet and natural world, especially the high mountain hiking and ski trails in the Canadian Rockies, for inspiring me and re-energizing me.

To spirit, when I get out of my own way, you show up with love and opportunity.

To our shared future.

Notes

1. The Dawn of System Leadership by Peter Senge, Hal Hamilton, & John Kania published in the Stanford Social Innovation Review Winter 2015. http://www.ssireview.org/articles/entry/the_dawn_of_system_leadership

2. http://gao.gov/assets/670/660952.pdf

3. Wikipedia (is a collaboration). http://en.wikipedia.org/wiki/Yin_and_yang

4. Cisco Blog, The Platform, Collaboration: What Does It Really Mean? by Carlos Dominguez, February 9, 2011. (Dominguez, 2011)

5. "The Dawn of System Leadership," by The Dawn of System Leadership published in the Stanford Social Innovation Review Winter 2015. http://www.ssireview.org/articles/entry/the_dawn_of_system_leadership (Kaufer, 2015)

6. McKinsey Quarterly, The Eight Essentials of Innovation; Strategic and Organizational Factors are what separate successful big-company innovators from the rest of the field, April 2015 by Marc de Jong, Nathan Marston, and Erik Roth. http://www.mckinsey.com/insights/innovation/the_eight_essentials_of_innovation?cid=other-eml-nsl-mip-mck-oth-1505 (Marc de Jong, 2015)

7. Wikinomics: How Mass Collaboration Changes Everything, Dan Tapscott and Anthony D. Williams

8. Alan D. MacCormack http://www.hbs.edu/faculty/Pages/profile.aspx?facId=6503

9. His Holiness, the Dalai Lama, How to be Compassionate, 2011

10. Gil Fronsdale, Insight Meditation Centre, California

11. The Silo Mentality: How To Break Down The Barriers by Brent Gleeson and Megan Rozo, published on Forbes.com October 2, 2013.

12. By pluralverse, I mean to define the complexity and diversity of the world. There is a pluralverse in our universe.

13. Margaret Wheatly http://margaretwheatley.com/

14. Dan Ardi http://corporateanthropologyadvisors.com/

15. Douglas Stone, Author of Difficult Conversations and Thanks for the Feedback, Boston, Massachusetts.

16. Nine Domains http://www.ninedomains.com/

17. Anthony Williams and Dan Tapscott, who wrote Radical Openness: Four Unexpected Principles for Success

18. Difficult Conversations: How to Discuss What Matters Most, Douglas Stone, Bruce Patton and Sheila Heen

19. Eric Ariel Fox http://www.winningfromwithin.com/

20. Enneagram Institute https://www.enneagraminstitute.com/

21. Bill Ury http://www.williamury.com/books/the-power-of-a-positive-no/

22. Martin Niemöller https://en.wikipedia.org/wiki/First_they_came_...

23. Rage Against the Machine http://www.ratm.com/

24. Heart and Stroke Foundation of Canada http://www.heartandstroke.com/

25. Manhatten Project http://www.pitt.edu/~sdb14/atombomb.html

26. Alberta Energy Regulator http://www.aer.ca/

27. Tamarack Institute http://tamarackcommunity.ca/

28. eKnow http://www.e-know.ca/

29. Power to the People https://www.youtube.com/watch?v=RtvlBS4PMF0

30. TransCanada Trail http://tctrail.ca/

31. Luke Dormehl http://www.lukedormehl.com/

32. Economist Intelligence Unit http://graphics.eiu.com/files/ad_pdfs/Business%20 2010_Global_FINAL.pdf

33. EdX and Google https://www.insidehighered.com/news/2013/09/11/edx-and-google-develop-open-source-mooc-platform

34. Mark Leslie: Putting the "We" in Leadership http://www.gsb.stanford.edu/insights/mark-leslie-putting-we-leadership

35. Scott Adams, creator of Dilbert.

36. Centre for Action and Contemplation https://cac.org/

37. Quiet: The Power of Introverts in a World that Can't Stop Talking http://www.quietrev.com/

38. Stephen Covey, The 7 Habits of Highly Effective People https://www.stephen-covey.com/7habits/7habits-habit7.php

39. Margaret J. Wheatley http://margaretwheatley.com/books-products/books/leadership-new-science/

40. ESCAPE http://ucalgary.ca/utoday/issue/2015-02-12/researchers-find-new-therapy-dramatically-benefits-stroke-patients

41. Heart and Stroke Foundation announcement on ESCAPE http://www.heartand-stroke.com/site/c.ikIQLcMWJtE/b.9253827/k.617E/Research_breakthrough_to_revolutionize_stroke_treatment.htm

42. ReThink Stakeholder Engagement and Regulatory Processes https://www.you-tube.com/watch?v=GSEDz5IqCi4

43. Rotary Four Way Test https://www.rotary.org/myrotary/en/learning-reference/about-rotary/guiding-principles

44. Linkage, Phil Harkins   http://www.linkageinc.com/leadership-development-documents/files/content/10-Leadership-Techniques-for-Building-High-Perfor-ming-Teams.pdf

45. Savage's Embrace Conflict Podcast http://www.voiceamerica.com/episode/88177/embrace-conflict

46. Peloton definition https://en.wikipedia.org/wiki/Peloton

47. Learning to Lead, Bennis and Goldsmith https://www.goodreads.com/book/show/171922.Learning_to_Lead

48. Jonathan Webb, Forbes.com http://www.forbes.com/sites/jwebb/2015/11/23/why-supplier-collaboration-projects-keep-hitting-the-wall/

49. Rockyview Development article http://www.canada.com/vancouversun/news/westcoastnews/story.html?id=2ead77da-5e03-418d-bde4-6c3eb1aadf01

50. World Café https://en.wikipedia.org/wiki/World_Cafe

51. East Hill Property for Sale http://www.dailytownsman.com/breaking_news/262388071.html

52. Margaret Wheatly quotes https://www.brainyquote.com/quotes/quotes/m/margaretj283904.html

53. Bhopal https://en.wikipedia.org/wiki/Bhopal_disaster

54. Art of Convening http://heartlandcircle.com/aocbook.htm

55. John Michel http://blogs.hbr.org/2014/08/great-leadership-isnt-about-you/

56. Stephen Hobbs http://wellthmovement.com/

57. Kenneth Cloke http://kennethcloke.com/

58. Theory of U http://www.ottoscharmer.com/

59. The main purpose of a Settlement Conference is to encourage the parties to a lawsuit to settle the lawsuit and avoid the time, anxiety and cost of a trial. See, for example, http://thelawcentre.ca/self_help/small_claims_factsheets/fact_12

60. Echart Tolle http://www.eckharttolle.com/books/newearth/

61. Hugh Landerkin http://www.aija.org.au/NAJ%202010/Papers/Landerkin%20H.pdf

62. Mind Up http://thehawnfoundation.org/mindup/

63. MindUp see; http://thehawnfoundation.org/mindup/

64. Centered Leadership http://www.mckinsey.com/client_service/organization/latest_thinking/centered_leadership

65. Einstein quotes https://www.brainyquote.com/quotes/quotes/a/alberteins110208.html

66. Brahmavihara https://en.wikipedia.org/wiki/Brahmavihara

67. Why Managers Haven't Embraced Complexity https://hbr.org/2013/05/why-managers-havent-embraced-c/

68. American Icon http://www.npr.org/books/titles/148292493/american-icon-alan-mulally-and-the-fight-to-save-ford-motor-company

69. Paul Harris https://www.rotary.org/en/about-rotary/history

70. Dan Pontrefact http://www.forbes.com/sites/danpontefract/

71. Economist Insight on Collaboration http://graphics.eiu.com/marketing/pdf/Cisco%20Collaboration.pdf

72. Attachment Theory http://www.simplypsychology.org/bowlby.html

73. Dee Ann Turner http://elevatepub.com/books/its-my-pleasure

74. see www.chuckrose.ca for Win or Walk Away, We Are One and more great music and leadership development.

75. When Internal Collaboration is Bad for Your Company https://hbr.org/2009/04/when-internal-collaboration-is-bad-for-your-company/ar/1

76. The Invisible Gorilla https://www.youtube.com/watch?v=oMg7Tmryzgk

77. Inattentional Blindness https://mitpress.mit.edu/index.php?q=books/inattentional-blindness

78. Meme https://en.wikipedia.org/wiki/Meme

79. Mapping the Value of Employee Collaboration http://www.mckinsey.com/insights/organization/mapping_the_value_of_employee_collaboration

80. Mumuration http://www.isciencetimes.com/articles/6725/20140123/murmuration-starlings-dance-sky-perfect-unison.htm

81. Keystone XL decision http://www.nytimes.com/2015/01/09/us/senate-panel-approves-keystone-pipeline-bill.html?_r=0

82. Collaboration is a Billion $ Industry http://www.fastcompany.com/1836468/why-your-company-needs-chief-collaboration-officer

83. Business Daily News Dani Ardi http://www.businessnewsdaily.com/5103-share-leadership-theory.html